Costume *Jewelry*

Identification and Price Guide

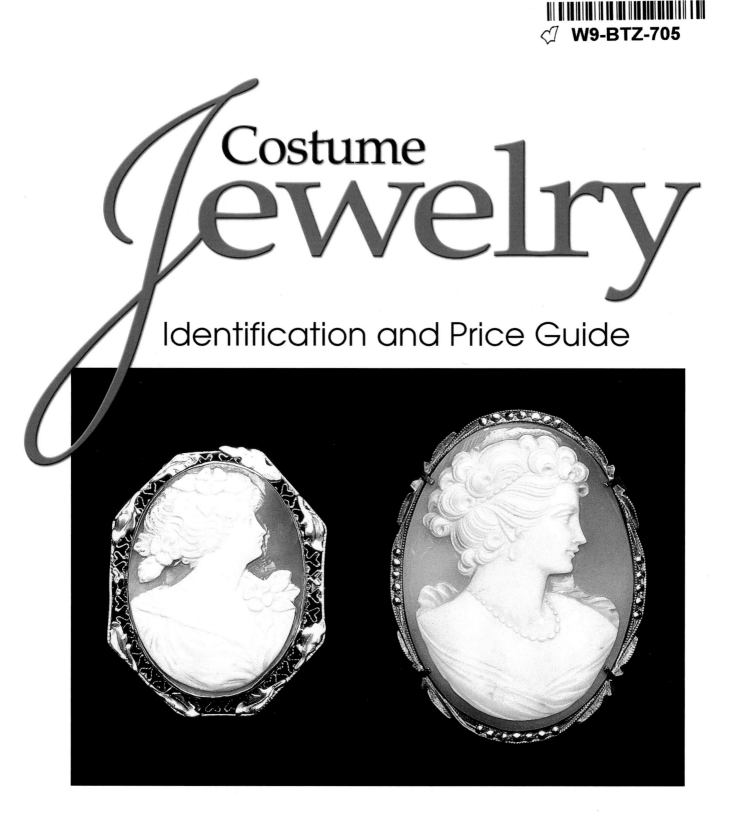

Leigh Leshner

©2004 Leigh Leshner
Published by

kp **krause publications**
An imprint of F+W Publications, Inc.

700 East State Street • Iola, WI 54990-0001
715-445-2214 • 888-457-2873
www.krause.com

Our toll-free number to place an order or obtain
a free catalog is (800) 258-0929.

Library of Congress Catalog Number: 2004090919

ISBN: 0-87349-826-7

Designed by Rebecca Robinson
Edited by Tracy Schmidt

Printed in the United States of America

Acknowledgments

I wish to thank my parents, Robert and Carol Leshner, for their undying support and unconditional love.

Thanks also to: Vintage Fashion and Costume Jewelry editor Lucille Tempesta and author Marcia Brown for their editorial expertise; Marcia Brown, Louise Champion, Gail Enos, Sheryl Hamilton, Karen Kennedy, Carol Leshner, Kristin Martinez, Skip and Patricia Peterson, and Adrienne Shivers for providing jewelry from their private collections; my editor Tracy Schmidt, page designer Rebecca Robinson, and acquisitions editor Paul Kennedy.

Special thanks go to Maurice Childs for his extraordinary photography.

Table of Contents

Introduction

Costume jewelry is an art form unto itself. Each piece is representative of not only the designer's imagination, but of the culture and customs of the times. History plays an important role in the creation, and is helpful in determining a piece's age. Over time the invention of materials and mechanisms has aided in the evolution, and has given designers the ability to perfect this art form.

When looking at a piece of jewelry, the elements can often provide clues to determine the age of each piece. Fashion and jewelry are closely related. The clothing of the times provides valuable information to date jewelry, because often jewelry is made to enhance clothing. It reflects cultural and economic developments, cultures and customs, and even religious beliefs. By learning to interpret these clues and becoming your own private investigator, you can unlock the mysteries surrounding the pieces already in your collection and others that you find on your quest for jewels. For example, the aurora borealis rhinestone was created in 1955, so a piece with an aurora borealis rhinestone could not have been made before 1955. Other dates of significance are:

1850—patent granted for the tube-shaped safety catch for pins

1894—patent granted for the screwback earring

1901—patent granted for the lever safety catch

1934—patent granted for the clipback earring finding

Costume jewelry is generally divided into periods and styles. A circa date is only an approximation. It includes the period of ten years preceding and proceeding the circa date. Each period may have several styles with some of the same styles and types of jewelry being made in both precious and non-precious materials. Additionally, there are recurring style revivals which are interpretations of styles from an earlier period such as Egyptian revival in the early- and late-1800s, and then again in the 1920s.

This book will be covering the styles and types of jewelry worn from the Victorian period through the mid-twentieth century. This book will cover jewelry that is available and accessible. Items that you might find at antique stores, antique shows, flea markets, garage sales, auctions, and on the internet. There might even be pieces that you already have in your own jewelry box!

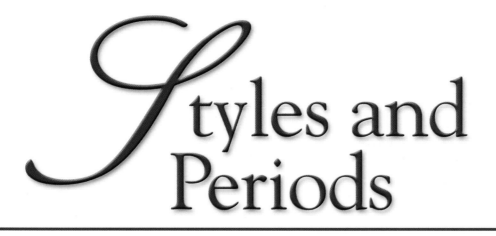

Styles and Periods

Victorian: 1837-1901

The Victorian period was named after Queen Victoria of England. She ascended the throne in 1837, and remained Queen until her death in 1901. The Victorian period is a long and prolific one; abundant with many styles of jewelry that warrant its being divided into three sub-periods: Early or Romantic period dating from 1837-1860; Mid or Grand period dating from 1860-1880; and Late or Aesthetic period dating from 1880-1901.

Queen Victoria loved jewelry. Her husband Albert gave her an engagement ring in the shape of a snake, which symbolized eternal love and good luck. Sentiment and romance was a significant factor in Victorian jewelry. Often, symbols within jewelry and clothing represented love and affection. On the couple's 6th anniversary, Albert gave Victoria a wreath for her hair made with orange blossoms. Each blossom represented one of their children.

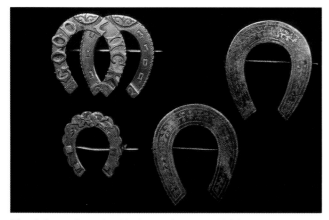

Top left: sterling double horseshoe good luck pin, c.1880, $145; bottom left: sterling horseshoe pin, c. 1890, $110; right: pair of horseshoe pins, steel with gold, c. 1850, $185.

Queen Victoria received other pieces of jewelry with symbolic motifs such as hearts, crosses, hands, flowers, anchors, doves, crowns, knots, stars, thistles, wheat, garlands, horseshoes and moons. The materials of the times were also abundant and varied. They included silver, gold, diamonds, onyx, glass, cameos, paste, carnelian, agate, coral, amber, garnet, emeralds, opals, pearls, peridot, rubies, sapphires, marcasites, cut steel, enameling, tortoise shell, topaz, turquoise, bog oak, ivory, jet, hair, gutta-percha, and vulcanite. Many of these motifs and materials have significant hidden meaning:

- **snake:** eternal love, good luck, eternity, wisdom
- **clasped hands:** friendship
- **coral:** wards off evil and danger
- **amethyst:** protection and good luck
- **bloodstone:** preserves health and stops bleeding
- **amber:** protects against disease
- **moonstones:** love, romance, and passion
- **peridot:** power to overcome timidity
- **pearls:** tears
- **horseshoes:** good luck
- **ivy:** friendship
- **forget-me-nots:** remembrance
- **silver coins:** love tokens
- **the term "Mizpah":** the Lord watch between me and thee when we are absent one from another.
- **"REGARD":** the first letter of each stone spelled out the word "Regard," for example, ruby, emerald, garnet, amethyst, ruby, and diamond. This was a token of affection.

Gold-filled slide bracelet with seed pearl, c. 1870, $210.

In 1830, the Industrial Revolution was in full swing. Jewelry could now be machine made. With the invention of electroplating in 1840, the use of rolled gold plating became prevalent. Gold-filled bangles, bracelets with tassels, hinged hollow bangles, and slide bracelets were worn by women. Often, the depressions in the engraved bangles were filled with black powdered enamel, fired, and then polished. This method was known as taille d'épargne.

Example of book chain necklace links.

The bookchain necklace was also a common motif. The necklaces were known as bookchains since the stamped rectangular folded over links resembled a book. Lockets were added to finish the necklace.

During the 1840s and 1850s, clothing accentuated the hourglass curves of a woman's body. Corsets were worn to give a fitted, tiny waist with an emphasis on the bust. Women wore full skirts and petticoats. During the daytime, women wore blouses with long sleeves, high necks, and lace collars often accented with brooches at the throat. In the evening, dresses were low cut with the arms exposed. By 1855, the necklines were lower and necklaces came into fashion.

Back view of cut steel.

Cut steel was used to make buckles, pins, necklaces, rings, and bracelets. Cut steel can be distinguished by its riveted and faceted beads, which are made from a thin metal and then applied to another metal plate. The steel is then cut into a design. The beads shine and sparkle from the light reflecting off of the facets. With the advent of industrialization, later versions of imitation cut steel were made by stamping the beads from a sheet of metal. To distinguish between cut steel and imitation cut steel, look at the back of the piece. If there are two pieces of metal, and one of the pieces is a solid plate with the rivets showing, that is a clue that the piece is old cut steel.

Left: tortoiseshell ring with sterling accents, c.1880, $345; right: tortoiseshell cameo brooch with piqué, c. 1870, $465.

The Victorians used natural materials in their jewelry designs. Tortoiseshell, a natural plastic, was used to make lockets, hair combs, bracelets, and brooches. Often, a method known as piqué was implemented. Piqué is a technique of decorating the tortoiseshell with a fine inlay of gold or silver metal that is heated and then pressed into the tortoiseshell.

Miniature, hand-painted portrait on porcelain in jet frame, c. 1830, $650.

Sentiments of love were often expressed in miniatures. Miniatures are often portraits of a loved one. Sometimes they were representative of deceased persons, but often the miniatures were of the living. Occasionally, the miniatures depicted landscapes, cherubs, or religious themes.

Louis J. M. Daguerre invented a photo process that led to the advent of photography. With the ability to take pictures of loved ones, jewelry that incorporated these photos soon followed. Photographs were inserted into brooches by being placed under glass. Some of the brooches were two sided, with one side housing the photograph and the other housing a lock of the loved one's hair.

Top left: Pietra-dura brooch in sterling frame, c.1920, $175; top right: Pietra-dura brooch in 800 silver frame, c.1920, $175; bottom right: Pietra-dura ring set in sterling with Art Nouveau design, c.1920, $145.

Italian artisans created souvenirs that served as both works of art and mementos. These artisans used two ancient techniques to create these pieces: mosaics and cameo carvings. There are two kinds of mosaics: Roman and Pietra-dura. Roman mosaics are made of small pieces of colored glass that when put together look like a miniature painting, usually depicting landscapes, archaeological ruins, or religious motifs. Pietra-dura is comprised of thin slices of colored stone that are cut to fit together to form a picture, often depicting flowers or birds.

Cameos are a miniature sculpture in relief. They are generally carved from a single stone where the background is cut away to make a design in relief. Many different materials have been used for cameos including onyx, agate, sardonyx, carnelian, coral, lava, jet, and shell. The earlier cameos were made from hardstone, and are the more sought after and collectible of the cameos. The most desirable of the hardstone cameos are ones made of agate. These cameos often have three to four layers of color. The hair may be one color, the skin another color, the dress a third color, and the background a fourth color. The carvers used the natural layers of the stone for the background and the foreground. Cameos carved from lava were popular tourist items at the ruins of Pompeii at Mount Vesuvius. While the cameos are often referred to as lava cameos, the material is actually a form of limestone that is mixed with

volcanic particles. As the demand for cameos increased, carvers turned to shell as it was less expensive to produce and less labor intensive.

When evaluating a cameo, the detail of the carving and the subject matter are significant in determining the value and the age. You should be able to see details such as strands of hair. There should be no chips or cracks, which can be found by holding the piece up to the light to check for damage. Classic Greek and Roman profiles and motifs were carved in the cameos of the early- to mid-Victorian periods. Often the hairstyles and clothing of the women in profile provide clues to a piece's age. A cameo can sometimes be dated by the shape of the woman's nose in profile. The Romanesque or aquiline noses are usually found on cameos of the mid-nineteenth century, while the pert turned up nose is usually found on later cameos.

There are other clues that can help determine age. If the point of the pin extends past the body of the cameo, it is generally a sign that it is an older cameo. If there is a safety catch, unless the clasp has been replaced, the cameo was likely made in the twentieth century, since the safety catch was not available until 1901. If the piece is plated, it was made after 1849 when gold electroplating was invented. Early Victorian cameos had simple frames, while the turn-of-the-century and Art Deco cameos often used filigree and white gold for a more delicate look.

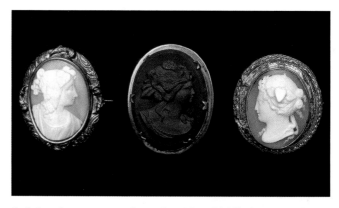

Left: hardstone cameo brooch with gold-filled engraved frame, c.1860, $450; middle: hardstone cameo brooch with gold-filled frame, c.1880, $195; right: shell cameo brooch with gold-filled frame, c.1900, $325.

Left: woven hair bracelet with photograph, missing glass and minor wear to hairwork, c. 1870, $225; right: gold-filled pin with woven hair, minor damage to one of the dangling charms, c.1870, $195.

Hair jewelry was a popular form of jewelry that was an expression of love and sentiment. The jewelry was a way to keep the loved one near to you. The hair of a loved one was placed in a special compartment in a brooch or a locket, or used to form a picture under the glass compartment. Later in the mid-nineteenth century, pieces of jewelry were made completely of woven hair. Individual strands of hair would be woven together to create necklaces, watch chains, brooches, earrings, and rings. Hair jewelry became so popular that at the Crystal Palace Exposition in 1853, a full line of hair jewelry was exhibited. Soon, merchants of hair jewelry were selling their wares at art fairs and markets throughout Europe. In the United States, soldiers would leave a lock of their hair with loved ones when they left for the Civil War. Godey's Lady's Book of 1850 stated, "Hair is at once the most delicate and last of our materials and survives us like love. It is light, so gentle, so escaping from the idea of death, that, with a lock of hair belonging to a child or friend we may almost look up to heaven and compare notes with angelic nature, may almost say, I have a piece of thee here, not unworthy of thy being now…"

The details of Victoria's life influenced the jewelry of the times. In 1848, Victoria purchased Balmoral as her summer home in Scotland. The craze for everything Scottish manifested itself into Scottish pebble jewelry. This type of jewelry reflected the romanticism of the Scottish lochs and the mysteries of the highlands. The jewelry consisted of multicolored agates set in silver or gold with Scottish motifs such as the thistle, dirk, and St. Andrew's cross. As this type of jewelry gained in popularity, new themes were added including the lover's knot, sheaths, arrows, bows, butterflies, padlocks, and snakes. The jewelry was made with a wide variety of stones including jasper, carnelian, banded onyx, moss agate, citrine, cairngorm, and amethyst.

In 1861, Prince Albert died causing Victoria to go into mourning for the rest of her life. Victoria required that the royal court wear black. This atmosphere spread to the populace and created a demand for mourning jewelry. Mourning jewelry is another form of sentimentalism. It is a memento to remember a loved one.

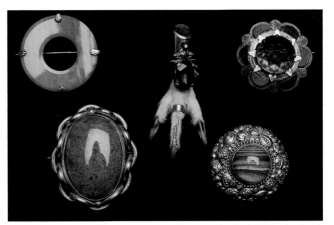

Top left: sterling brooch with agate, c.1880, $225; top right: sterling target brooch with agate, jasper and cairngorms, c.1860, $425; middle: sterling grouse pin with amethyst, c.1860, $365; bottom left: agate brooch set in gold-filled rope frame, c.1900, $145; bottom right: sterling brooch with banded agate, c.1880, $160.

Mourning jewelry is typically black. When it first came into fashion, it was made from jet. Jet is a fossilized coal that was mined in Whitby, England. By 1850, there were fifty workshops that used jet to make brooches, lockets, bracelets, and necklaces. As the supply of jet dwindled, other materials were used such as vulcanite, gutta-percha, bog oak and French jet. French jet should not be confused with true jet because French jet is glass. It is easy to tell the difference between the two materials as French jet is cool to the touch and is a heavier and harder substance than jet, which is room temperature and lightweight.

Left: vulcanite bracelet strung on black elastic, c.1850, $345; right: jet bangle, c.1860, $395.

Vulcanite is a hardened rubber. Pieces made of vulcanite are molded rather than carved. When rubbed, vulcanite smells like burnt rubber. Another telltale sign of vulcanite is that it will fade to dark brown with exposure to sunlight, while jet will stay true to its black color.

By the 1880s, the dark, gloomy, and somber mourning jewelry was losing popularity. Mourning had become relaxed, and fashions had changed. The clothing was simpler and had an air of delicacy. The Industrial Revolution, which began in the early part of the century, was now in full swing and machine manufactured jewelry was affordable to the working class. Machine-made, die-stamped jewelry was a popular form of showing sentiment. Common motifs included horseshoes, animals, stars, crescents, birds, lizards, Japanese motifs, message brooches, hearts, and flowers.

Edwardian: 1890-1920

The turn of the century was a time of change. Though Edward VII ascended the throne in 1901, he and his wife Alexandria of Denmark exerted influence over the style for the ten-year period before, and after, his ascension. The 1890s was known as La Belle Epoque. This was a time known for ostentation and extravagance. Women wore big hats festooned with large feathers and plumes of all shades. The jewelry they wore accented this bold display of style. As the years moved on, the lines became simpler. The jewelry became smaller. Instead of wearing one large brooch, women were often found wearing several small lapel pins.

Into the 1900s, extravagance was again in vogue. Luxurious fabrics, sequins, beads, and lace were used in clothing. Platinum, diamonds, and pearls were prevalent in the jewelry of the wealthy, while paste was being used by the masses to imitate the real thing. The styles were reminiscent of the neo-classical and rococo styles. The jewelry was lacy, ornate, feminine, and delicate. Diamond and pearl dog collars and festoon necklaces made of precious metals and gemstones were popular among the upper class while the working class popularized dog collars and festoon necklaces made

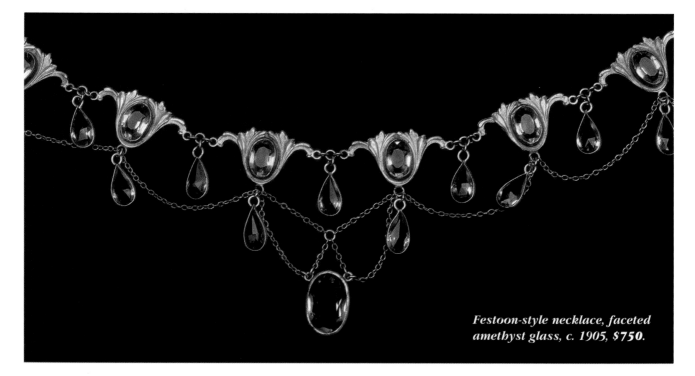

Festoon-style necklace, faceted amethyst glass, c. 1905, $750.

of pot metal, glass and rhinestones, lavalieres, delicate gold and gold-filled pins, and filigree pins and bracelets. Two popular styles of necklaces, the negligee and the sautoir, were carried on into the designs of the Art Deco period of the 1920s. A negligee is a necklace that has a pendant drop suspended from unequal lengths of chain. A sautoir is a long necklace with a tassel or pendant at the end of the chain or rope. Some common motifs of this period are good luck symbols, horseshoes, wishbones, doves, hearts, wreaths, ribbons, bows, flowers, garlands, fish, peacocks, stars, and moons. Common materials included pearls, diamonds, amethysts, peridot, garnet, ruby, sapphire, emerald, opal, platinum, silver, white gold, pot metal, rhinestones, and glass.

Art Nouveau: 1895-1910

*Left: sterling Wm. B Kerr brooch, c. 1905, **$850**; right: sterling pendant on chain, c. 1895, **$225.***

In 1895, Samuel Bing opened a shop called "L'Art Nouveau" at 22 Rue de Provence in Paris, France. He is credited with starting the Art Nouveau movement. His shop carried the designs of Louis Comfort Tiffany and Rene Lalique. Art Nouveau was influenced by the aestheticism of the late nineteenth century. The designs of the jewelry were characterized by a sensuality of the designs. Jewelry took on the forms of the female figure, butterflies, dragonflies, peacocks, snakes, wasps, swans, bats, orchids, irises, and other exotic flowers. The lines were not angular. Instead, the designers used whiplash curves and exaggerated and stylized lines to create a feeling of lushness and opulence. Two popular American firms were Unger Brothers and William Kerr and Co.

Various materials were used including horn, ivory, tortoiseshell, carved glass, opals, moonstones, quartz, amethysts, carnelian, garnet, lapis, malachite, mother-of-pearl, gold, and silver. The use of rhinestones was limited. The stones were used to accent the jewelry rather than overpower it. Lockets were adorned with small rhinestones in a variety shades. Clear rhinestones were used to imitate diamonds while colored stones were used to resemble gemstones such as rubies, sapphires, and emeralds. Sash ornaments were accented with rhinestones in varying sizes. Often, the rhinestones were mixed with other materials such as faceted glass and faux pearls.

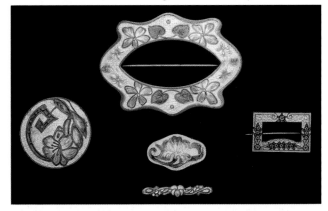

*Top: brass enameled sash ornament/pin, c. 1895, **$195**; middle left: brass enamel floral pin, c. 1895, **$95**; middle: sterling enamel pin , c. 1895, **$125**; middle right: sterling enamel pin, c. 1895, **$125**; bottom: brass enamel pin, c. 1895, **$85**.*

Enameling was a popular technique used during this time. Enamel is a glass-like mixture of silica, quartz, borax, feldspar, lead, and metallic oxides. The mixture is ground into a powder and then applied to the piece of jewelry. It is then fired so that the mixture melts and adheres to the metal. There are several different types of enameling: plique-à-jour, basse-taille, champlevé, and cloisonné. Plique-à-jour is similar to stained glass. It is done without a backing, and the enameling is translucent. Basse-taille is translucent enamel, which is fired over an engraved or designed piece of metal and then polished. Champlevé is a technique where enamel is poured into designs that are cut into the metal and then fired and polished. Cloisonné is done by drawing the design and then outlining the design with fine gold wire. The enamel is then poured into the compartments, fired, and polished.

Sterling butterfly necklace with coral, c. 1910, $750.

Arts & Crafts: 1890-1920

Similar to the theory behind the Art Nouveau movement, the Arts & Crafts movement was focused on the aesthetic appeal of a piece of jewelry. The heart of the movement was with artisans and handcraftsmanship. There was a simplification of form where the material was secondary to the design and craftsmanship. The pieces were simple and, at times, abstract. They were handmade, hand hammered, patinated, and acid etched. Common materials were brass, bronze, copper, silver, blister pearls, freshwater pearls, turquoise, agate, opals, moonstones, coral, horn, ivory, base metals, amber, cabochon-cut garnets and amethysts.

In Chicago, the Kalo Shop (1900-1970) was a maker of jewelry and metal ware that used sterling, blister pearls, abalone, coral, shell, and moonstones in its designs. In Boston, the Society of Arts and Crafts used stones and metal rather than enameling in its designs. In Buffalo, NY, the Heintz Art Metal Shop was known for its use of patinated bronze with sterling overlay in cutout patterns on its jewelry and metal ware. Other names to look for are the Art Silver Shop, T.C. Shop, James H. Winn, Lebolt & Co., and Marcus & Co.

In Germany, Theodor Fahrner was known for his interpretations of the "Jugendstil" movement, which was the German term for the Arts & Crafts movement. The company employed many designers, some of whom signed their pieces. The signature for Fahrner is a TF in a circle, which the company began using in 1901, even though the company was founded in 1855.

In Halifax, Great Britain, Charles Horner was known for his small pins, hatpins, and brooches, which incorporated the use of silver and enamel. He signed his work C.H.

Liberty and Co of London became famous for its mass-produced interpretations of handmade pieces. The company hired artisans to create pieces which the company would then machine make, but hand finish. The company's principal designer was Archibald Knox. Another designer who is of interest from this period is William Haseler, who signed his pieces WHH, from Birmingham, England.

1920s and 1930s

During the 1920s, the fashion of the times was changing. World War I had an effect on clothing designs. The style went from tight, narrow, floor-length skirts to fuller, shorter hemlines. Curves had been abandoned in favor of more loose fitting, drop-waisted dresses. There were two distinct styles of the twenties: the feminine style and the androgynous style, often referred to as the jeune-fille look. This style emphasized a modern look for the time that was a loose, straight cut de-emphasizing the hourglass figure of a woman's body. The clothing had become lighter and more ornate. Dresses were accented with beads and fringe. Women began bobbing their hair, which led to the adornment of chandelier-type earrings. Low-cut dress lines were accompanied by sautoirs, flapper beads, and chokers, which drew attention to the décolletage.

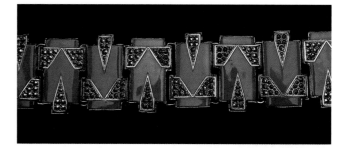

Czechoslovakian Art Deco bracelet with blue glass and marcasites, c. 1925, $395.

These fashions were often accompanied by jewelry that drew on the Art Deco movement. The Art Deco movement, 1920-1935, got its beginning in Paris at the Exposition Internationale des Arts Decoratifs et Industriales Modernes. The idea behind this movement was that form follows function. The style was characterized by simple, straight, clean lines, stylized motifs, geometric shapes, and streamlined curves. Zigzag designs and sharp angles accented by colored stones and strong contrasting colors were in vogue. Materials often used were chrome, rhodium, pot metal, glass, rhinestones, Bakelite, and celluloid.

Czechoslovakia is a country that has a history rich in glassmaking including hand-blown, molded, and cut glass. The center of Czechoslovakian jewelry production was Gablonz, where there had always been a tradition of glassmaking. Glass was not limited to functional objects. By 1918, the Czechoslovakian glass industry began to use innovative and creative techniques, which they incorporated into jewelry designs. Thousands of people worked out of their homes as glass pressers, grinders, and cutters to make perfume bottles, vanity items, beads, and rhinestones.

The rhinestones were manmade gemstones from highly refined glass. The glass is first colored by the introduction of various metals, and then it is pressed into molds to create the final shape. Each stone is ground and polished on all facets by machine to extract the brilliance. The stones are generally foiled. This opaque back coating increases the reflectivity and brilliance, while allowing the stone's back to be glued into the setting without seeing the glue. Oftentimes, rhinestones are referred to as paste. Originally, glass paste was glass that was ground into a paste, molded, and then melted. The final piece was an opaque, dense glass with a frosted surface. The paste would have numerous air bubbles and swirl marks, but the highly leaded glass was cut with facets to reflect the light and it was placed in a copper or silver lining. When the term paste is currently used, it generally refers to rhinestones. While the United States refers to the term rhinestone, the terms paste, strass, and diamente are often used in Europe.

Czechoslovakia produced jewelry that reflected the times. The opening of King Tut's tomb in 1922 led to an Egyptian revival in jewelry. Glass beads were made in Czechoslovakia that were molded to resemble pharaohs, sphinxes, and scarabs.

Czechoslovakian jewelry can often be identified through the use of a combination of enameling, rhinestones, and glass. The jewelry ranges from ornate to simple and refined. The country did not exist before World War I. Before that time, the area was known as Bohemia. This is another clue for the collector. If the piece is marked Czechoslovakia, you know that it could not have been made before 1918, since Czechoslovakia did not exist before that time.

Costume jewelry was an outgrowth of the average person's desire to have copies of the real jewelry that had previously been reserved for the wealthy. Costume jewelry began its steady ascent to popularity in the 1920s. Since it was relatively inexpensive to produce, there was mass production. The sizes and designs of the jewelry varied. Often, it was worn a few times, disposed of, and then replaced with a new piece. It was thought of as expendable, a cheap throwaway to dress up an outfit. Costume jewelry became so popular that it was sold in both the upscale fine stores as well as the "five and dime."

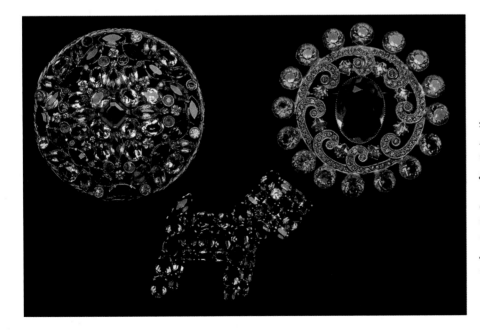

Left: Czechoslovakian brooch with red, pink, lavender, topaz, green and blue glass, c. 1930, $185; middle: Czechoslovakian dog brooch, purple glass and rhinestone, c. 1930, $145; right: Czechoslovakian brooch, blue glass and blue rhinestones, c.1935, $195.

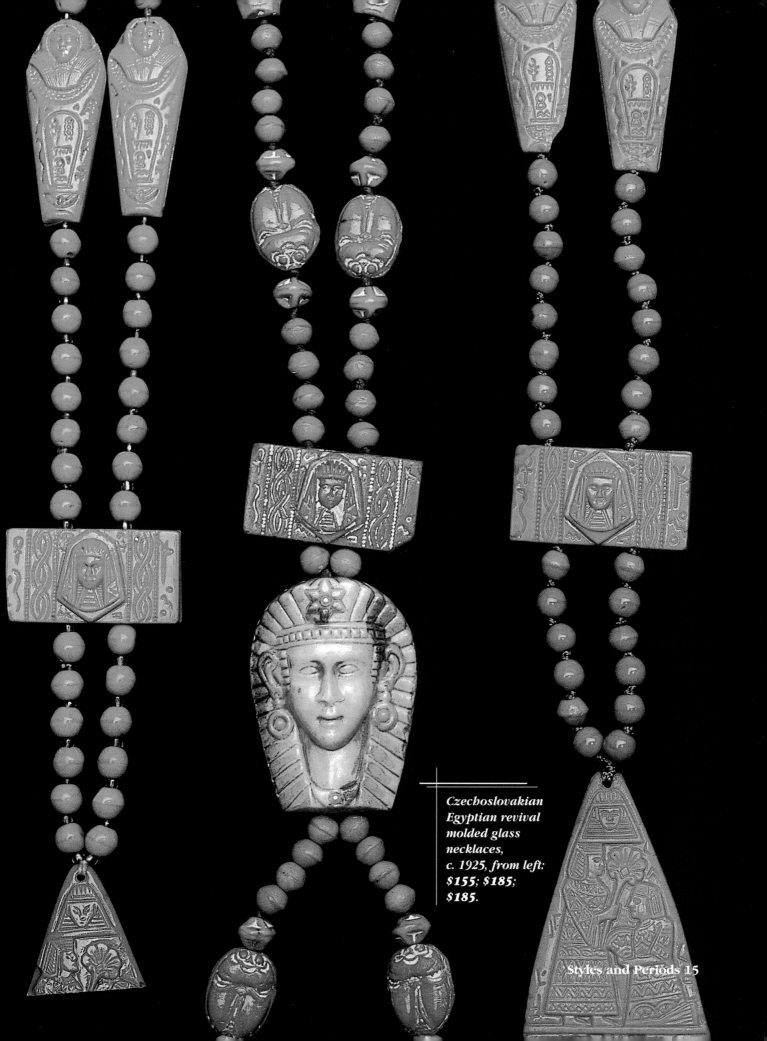

Czechoslovakian Egyptian revival molded glass necklaces, c. 1925, from left: $155; $185; $185.

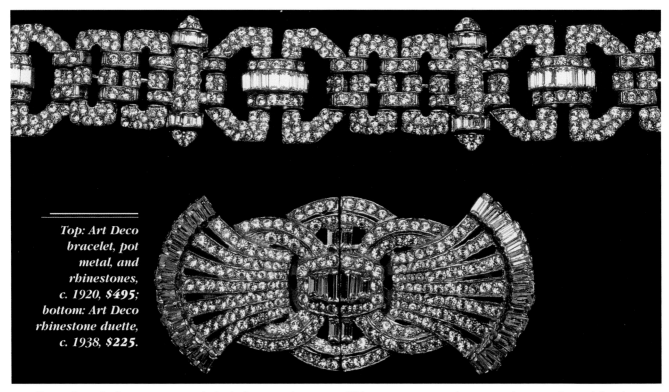

Top: Art Deco bracelet, pot metal, and rhinestones, c. 1920, $495; bottom: Art Deco rhinestone duette, c. 1938, $225.

Even though the cost was relatively low, each piece brought pleasure to its wearer. The designs had an intrinsic beauty that made them unique and special. The designs ranged from the subtle to the outrageous. Because of the relatively inexpensive production costs, designers were able to unleash their creativity while at the same time maintain high production standards. Many of the designers had a background in fine jewelry and they brought their knowledge and skill to this rather new phenomenon of "fake" jewelry. These were jewelers who were used to working with gemstones. They now were able to take their glorious designs and interpret them into costume jewelry for the average woman. The quality was unsurpassed and the designs were unique, and often rivaled their "real" counterparts.

One designer who played an important role not only in clothing design, but also in costume jewelry design, was Coco Chanel. She created costume jewelry to decorate her clothing. She knew the true meaning of the complete costume, and she began wearing her costume jewelry. Jewelry was generally reserved for evening wear, but Chanel wore it during the day, making it fashionable for millions of other women follow suit.

The 1920s is often called the "White Period."

This term was apt because the metal used for the jewelry was a variety of white metals such as pot metal and base metals, and the prevalent rhinestone used was a clear one. As the period progressed, the jewelry was created using bolder colors. The metal was accented with stones of a rainbow of colors in ruby, sapphire, emerald, black, amethyst, and topaz.

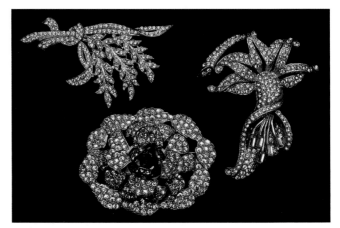

Top left: floral pot metal brooch with rhinestones, c. 1920, $152; bottom left: pot metal floral brooch with rhinestones, c. 1925, $195; right: three-dimensional, pot metal floral brooch with rhinestones, c. 1930, $115.

While many pieces were made by well-recognized designers and companies, a greater percentage of the jewelry was unsigned. These signed, as well as unsigned, pieces were works of art. The designers were free to express themselves in an unbridled fashion that was evident in the designs that ranged from whimsical to elegant. Just as with any other item, there was a wide range of quality in terms of the material used. Pieces ranged from low-end base metal to higher-end sterling. While the materials may have been different in terms of perceived quality, the finished product was a sight to behold. The designs included flowers, figurals, bows, Art Deco designs, animals, geometric designs, and much more. The designers not only used rhinestones to enhance the metal, but they incorporated molded glass, beads, faux pearls, and gemstones. Enameling techniques were often used to add color.

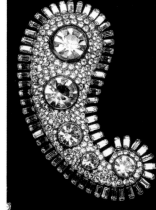

Dress clip.

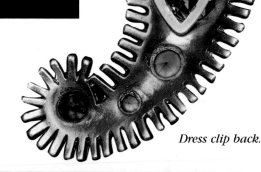

Dress clip back.

With the 1930s came the Depression and the advent of World War II. These world changes impacted society as a whole. Labor-intensive fashion was no longer economically viable. The designs began to move back to a more sculptured, softer, feminine look. Clothing was now functional and meant to last for a long time.

While life was often in turmoil, jewelry was one way to provide a respite. Women could purchase a relatively inexpensive piece of jewelry to make an old outfit look new. Designers began using enameling and brightly colored rhinestones to create wonderful whimsical designs of birds, flowers, circus animals, bows, dogs, and just about every other figural you could imagine. Through the use of enameling and colored rhinestones, the jewelry was bright and festive.

Dress clips were especially popular in the 1930s. Clips were made from precious materials such as platinum and diamonds to pot metal, plastics, wood, and rhinestones. Dress clips have a flat-hinged clip

Clockwise from top left: pot metal Clipmate, $155; Coro Duette, $180; Coro Duette. $165; and pot metal clipmate, $165.

with prongs that grasp the fabric to hold the clip in place.

In 1931, Coro patented the Duette and in 1936, Trifari patented the Clipmate. Both of these creations were brooches that consisted of two dress clips or fur clips that would come apart from the pin and could be worn separately or as one large brooch.

Styles and Periods 17

Retro: 1939-1950

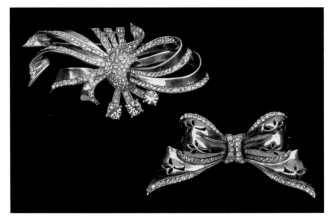

Left: sterling vermeil bow brooch, clear rhinestones, c. 1940, $265; right: sterling vermeil bow brooch, clear rhinestones, c. 1940, $195.

World War II impacted the world of fashion. Many European designers went into hiding or were sent to concentration camps, some of the couture houses closed their doors, and other designers immigrated to the United States. The exportation of European clothing was down, and domestic production was now at the forefront. The fashions were narrow and tailored with padded shoulders and nipped-in waists. The jewelry designs of the 1940s were big and bold. The jewelry had a more substantial feel to it, and designers began using larger stones to enhance the dramatic pieces. The jewelry was stylized and exaggerated. The designers indulged in their fantasies. Common motifs included flowing scrolls, bows, ribbons, birds, animals, snakes, flowers, and knots.

Due to World War II, the use of pot metal (the tin and lead used in pot metal) was prohibited for use other than for the military. Sterling now became the metal of choice, often dipped in a gold wash known as vermeil. The vermeil was done in yellow, pink, and rose gold.

Reflecting the world around them, the designers often created designs that had a militaristic feeling to it. The jewelry had themes of American flags, a v-sign for victory, Uncle Sam's hat, airplanes, anchors, and eagles. These creations were to be worn as a sign of support for the war effort, and those involved in the fight for freedom.

Trifari sterling bug, Lucite jelly belly with rhinestones and red cabochons, c. 1940s, $300.

Bakelite, celluloid, Lucite, and plastic were popular materials and no materials were wasted. As part of their war efforts, Trifari installed Plexiglas windshields and turrets in military bombers. However, the company would only use flawless materials, which resulted in the company being left with rejected material. Rather than throw away the leftovers, Alfred Phillipe, one of the designers, came up with the idea of cutting cabochons from the Plexiglas and incorporating them into jewelry designs. These designs are known as jelly bellies where the Lucite cabochons are the predominate feature of the whimsical line of jewelry which includes fish, spiders, elephants, bees, and other creatures.

1950s

Left: brooch, citrine and aurora borealis rhinestones, c. 1958, $25; right: earrings, orange aurora borealis rhinestones, c. 1958, $20.

The 1950s fashions had two distinct looks: elegant and sophisticated for the mature woman, and casual and fun for young people. Dior's "New Look" was prevalent with its narrow shoulders, small waists, and longer, fuller skirts. Accessories were prominent, with shoes, purses, gloves, belts, hats, and jewelry all coordinating. The young people wore jeans, t-shirts, tight sweaters, cardigans, beaded sweaters, pointed bras, and circular skirts. Jewelry that accessorized these outfits was fun and flirty.

The 1950s saw the rise of jewelry that was made purely of rhinestones. The stones had become the basis of necklaces, bracelets, earrings, and pins. A common term that is often heard when describing jewelry from the 1950s is prom jewelry. This term is used to describe necklaces, bracelets, and earrings that had smaller rhinestones prong set in metal with simplistic designs. Typically, this jewelry is not that valuable or collectible. Yet, this was only one type of rhinestone jewelry. Other pieces consisted of large, bold, multicolored rhinestones that were sold as sets of pins, earrings, necklaces, and bracelets.

In 1955, the aurora borealis rhinestone was introduced. By knowing when this stone was first made, a collector then knows that a piece of jewelry containing an aurora borealis stone could not have been made before 1955.

1960s

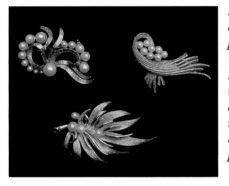

Left: goldtone brooch with faux pearls, c.1960s, $30; middle: Boucher brooch with faux pearls, c.1960s, $45; right: goldtone brooch with faux pearls, c.1960s, $20.

The focus of the early 1960s was on the average woman. Functional clothing was back in style with Jackie Kennedy providing the role model. Clean lines, pillbox hats, and A-line dresses with short jackets were a mainstay for the conservative woman. The large bold rhinestone pieces were no longer the must-have accessory. They were now replaced with smaller, more delicate gold-tone metal and faux pearls with only a hint of rhinestones.

At the other end of the spectrum was the beat collection, which consisted of psychedelic-colored clothing, Nehru jackets, thigh-high mini skirts, and go-go boots. These clothes were accessorized with beads, large metal pendants, and occasionally big, bold rhinestones. However, times were changing and by the late 1960s, there was the movement back to Mother Nature and the "hippie" look was born. Ethnic clothing, tie-dye, long skirts, fringe, and jeans were

the prevalent style, and the rhinestone had, for the most part, been thrown to the wayside.

From 1945-1965, there was a movement similar to the Arts & Crafts movement that emphasized the artistic approach to jewelry making. It is referred to as mid-century

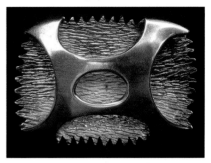

Sterling brooch, c. 1955, $285.

modern. This modernistic approach was occurring at a time when the beat generation was prevalent. These avant-garde designers created jewelry that was handcrafted to illustrate the artist's own concepts and ideas often manifesting themselves in abstract and modern designs. The pieces were unusual and abstract. The emphasis was on the design. The materials often used in the jewelry were sterling, gold, copper, brass, enamel, cabochons, wood, quartz, and amber.

While many of the pieces designed are unsigned or made by unknown artists, there are many artists whose pieces are sought after. They include:

Sam Kramer: Utilized odd materials and designed abstract, out-of-the-ordinary pieces. His signature is a mushroom inside a lobed circle.

Margaret De Patta: Her signature is a stylized "M" with a dot above it. Sometimes she also included her last name.

Paul Lobel: Opened a studio in 1944 in Greenwich Village. Utilized forged wire and silver sheet for his abstract figural designs. His jewelry is signed Lobel.

Art Smith: Created sculptural designs. He signed some, but not all, of his pieces.

Ed Weiner: Utilized silver and gold as well as some gemstones in his designs. He signed some of his pieces EW while some of his designs remained unsigned.

Ronald Pearson: Utilized forged or cast silver or gold for his uncomplicated designs.

Among the others to look for are Harry Bertoia, Jules Brenner, Alexander Calder, Betty Cooke, Ed Levin, Earl Pardon, Olaf Skoogfors, Henry Steig, Bill Tendler, Irene Brynner, Esther Lewittes, Franciso Rebaje, and Peter Macchiarini.

$\mathcal{S}$igned $\mathcal{C}$ostume Jewelry

Costume jewelry manufacturers were concentrated in New York and Providence, Rhode Island. In fact, Providence was coined the "Rhinestone Capital." Records show that in the late 1940s, 85 to 90 percent of the total jewelry output was being done in this city.

There are many wonderful manufacturers and designers of costume jewelry; designers that collectors have come to love and cherish. Unfortunately, to cover all of them would fill a library in and of itself.

The following companies are those whose names commonly appear when discussing signed costume jewelry:

BOUCHER

Marcel Boucher came to the United States from France in 1925. He began working in the jewelry trade as a designer for Cartier. He polished his skills before striking out on his own in 1937, with his Marboux line. This line was marked "MB" with a stylized Phrygian helmet that many people mistakenly call a rooster. The company produced 30 to 40 designs a week amounting to over 300 yearly creations. In 1940, the trademark "MB" was used. In the 1950s, the company began to use the Boucher name, and a design number was stamped separately on each piece. Early Boucher jewelry used bright enameling, colored stones, and was often of three-dimensional design. The jewelry was known for its quality and use of outstanding colored stones. Today, some of the more highly sought after Boucher pieces are his enameled birds and praying mantis brooches.

Boucher sterling vermeil brooch with blue and clear rhinestones, $425.

CHANEL

Coco Chanel began her career as a seamstress and hat designer in Paris. She opened her own shop in 1912, Chanel Modes. A woman could shop in her boutique for her whole wardrobe, from hats to jewelry to clothing to shoes. Chanel became so successful that by 1938, she was employing over 4,000 people in her houses of fine fashion. World War II forced her to close her doors for fifteen years, but she re-opened Chanel Modes in 1954, where she remained at the helm until her death in 1971. However, the doors to Chanel remain open and still carry on the tradition of quality and beauty that Chanel embodied. Much of the earlier Chanel jewelry is unsigned, while others are marked with a script "chanel."

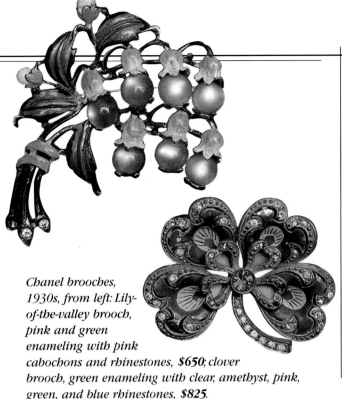

Chanel brooches, 1930s, from left: Lily-of-the-valley brooch, pink and green enameling with pink cabochons and rhinestones, $650; clover brooch, green enameling with clear, amethyst, pink, green, and blue rhinestones, $825.

CORO & COROCRAFT

One of the more prolific companies was Coro, which was created by Emmanuel Cohn and Carl Rosenberger in 1902. In the late 1920s, they built their own factory in Providence to become the leading manufacturer of costume jewelry in the United States. Over the decades, the company created numerous product lines that sold throughout the world. Factories were opened in the United Kingdom and in Canada to keep up with the massive production that was needed. Because of this large volume of production, Coro is easy to find. The company offered something for everyone, from the budget conscious shopper to the society matron.

Coro developed their Corocraft line in 1933 and continued production through the 1970s. This line was the higher-end jewelry often done in sterling vermeil featuring Art Deco, Art Nouveau designs, and figural jelly bellies.

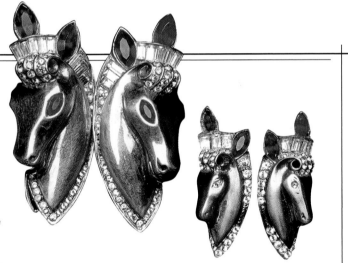

Coro sterling vermeil horse head Duette and matching earrings with clear and red rhinestones, $425.

EISENBERG

Jonas Eisenberg began his career in Chicago as a manufacturer of women's wear in 1880. His ready-to-wear fashions were unique, because they included a beautiful rhinestone brooch which was added to generate sales. These unsigned brooches were manufactured by wholesale firms, and added to complement the clothing. Soon however, stores began reporting that the jewelry was being stolen off of the dresses. Jonas' two sons, Samuel and Harold, who had taken over the company in 1914, soon realized that the rhinestone brooches were more popular than the clothing. The previously unmarked brooches now bore the name Eisenberg Originals. In 1935, Fallon and Kappel of New York was commissioned to create clothing accessories for the company. In 1937, the brothers began a separate jewelry line. Ruth M. Kamke was hired as one of their chief designers in 1940, and she continued to work there until 1972. She is credited

Eisenberg Original rhinestone dress clips, c. 1930s, $145.

with creating the Eisenberg Ice line, which got its name from the use of the sparkling rhinestones that were set to enhance their icy whiteness. By 1958, the clothing line was discontinued, but the jewelry line continued its prolific climb. While the later Eisenberg Ice line is collectible, it is the Eisenberg Originals that are the most sought after. These pieces were cast and the brilliant stones were handset creating beautiful and quality pieces.

MIRIAM HASKELL

In 1924, Miriam Haskell was running a gift shop in the McAlpin Hotel in New York City. She was making costume jewelry, and with the help of Frank Hess, she left the retail business and began wholesaling the jewelry. In the early days, Hess was the sole designer, with Haskell overseeing the production. Each piece was carefully made to maintain the beauty of the design. Typical Haskell jewelry is made of small faux seed pearls wired onto gilt filigree brass. She also used materials such as turquoise, glass, leather, shells, and coral. Though the company has changed hands over the years, the Haskell tradition of craftsmanship and beauty still continues today.

Miriam Haskell necklace and matching earring set with amethyst glass beads, blue glass, clear, and amethyst rhinestones, c. 1940s/1950s, $825.

HOBE

The Hobe family has been in the jewelry business for four generations. Patriarch Jacques Hobe was a Parisian master craftsman who designed jewelry, and was named a royal jeweler to the court of France. His son, William, apprenticed with him and after World War I, moved to California where he began designing buckles. In 1920, he moved to New York and started the Hobe Button Company. Joined by his wife, Sylvia Kittner, they designed jewelry and accessories for the Broadway production of "My Fair Lady," and began selling quality jewelry to the public. The reigns were then passed on to William's sons, Robert and Donald. The company designed for Hollywood stars, as well as the average housewife, by providing a standard of excellence and a look that mimicked the real thing without the expensive price.

Top: Hobe sterling bracelet with red rhinestones, $325; bottom: Hobe sterling floral brooch with blue rhinestone, $225.

HOLLYCRAFT

The Hollycraft jewelry company was founded in 1948 by Joseph Chorbagian, his cousin Archie, and Jack Hazard. The company was based in New York City. The first two years in business, the company simply marked the jewelry Hollycraft. The company was known for producing pieces in an antique gold finish that served as the background for distinctive pastel-colored rhinestones in wonderful shades of blues, greens, yellows, pinks, and lavenders. They were also known for their whimsical and novelty lines of jewelry, including Christmas-themed pieces and fruit. In 1950, the company began marking their jewelry with Hollycraft as well as the date of manufacture. The company discontinued business in the 1960s and was sold in 1972.

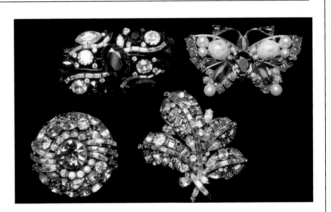

Hollycraft brooches, from top left; japanned metal with clear, aurora borealis, and dark green aurora borealis rhinestones, $145; butterfly with opaque cabochons, faux pearls, blue, lavender, green, topaz, and red rhinestones, $125; floral motif with lavender, citrine, light blue, light green, blue, pink, and clear rhinestones, $175; and circle with lavender, citrine, light blue, light green, blue, pink, and clear rhinestones, $165.

SCHIAPARELLI

Elsa Schiaparelli was born in Rome, Italy, but moved to France in the early 1920s, where she designed fine jewelry. In 1934, she opened her own house of fashion in Paris. Schiaparelli was enamored with color, and shocking pink became her signature color. Schiaparelli was the first person to offer high fashion ready-to-wear clothing. At the peak of her career in 1940, she employed over 350 seamstresses and assistants. American production of Schiaparelli began in 1949, and was handled by the Ralph DeRosa Company. She retired from business in 1954.

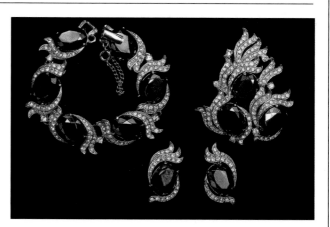

Schiaparelli brooch, bracelet and earring set, rhinestones, c.1950s, $495.

TRIFARI

Trifari was another prolific company. In 1924, Gustavo Trifari, a manufacturer and designer of hair ornaments and bar pins, and Leo Krussman, a salesman, joined forces. A year later they brought in partner Carl Fishel. Trifari/Krussman/Fishel were the first to use imported Austrian rhinestones. This led to their being known as the rhinestone kings. In 1930, Alfred Phillipe, a fine jeweler by trade, joined the company as head designer. He soon initiated the use of Swarovski multicolored rhinestones which were handset in the jewelry. Because of his background as a fine jeweler, his designs often rivaled those using gemstones. The company's earlier pieces had been marked TKF, which stood

Trifari necklace, brooch, hinged bangle, and earring with faux pearls, green and red cabochons, blue faceted glass, and clear rhinestones, $2,450.

for Trifari Krussman and Fishel. Later, however, the company decided to eliminate the use of the three last names in favor of Trifari.

WEISS

After apprenticing at Coro, Albert Weiss opened his own business in 1942. He recognized the importance of quality rhinestones, and he used Austrian rhinestones to give that extra sparkle to his jewelry. While most of the company's pieces are signed Weiss, the company sold unmarked jewelry to stores such as Sears and JC Penney. Weiss was the first designer to introduce the "black diamond," which is a smoky-colored stone that became popular among other designers. Besides creating exquisite rhinestone necklaces, earrings, bracelets,

and pins, Weiss was known for his Christmas tree pins, which are highly sought after collectibles. The company closed its doors in 1971 after three decades in business.

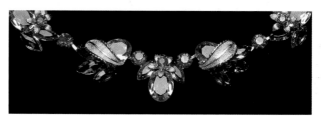

Weiss necklace with pink, fuchsia, and lavender rhinestones, $185.

Novelty Jewelry:
Bakelite, Celluloid, Lucite, Wood, and Ceramics

In the 1920s through the 1960s, new materials to jewelry making were used. Designers used celluloid, Bakelite, Lucite, wood, leather, and ceramics to create whimsical figurals, flowers, vegetables, animals, people, western themes, and geometric designs. These materials were relatively inexpensive, and could be used to make fun and fanciful jewelry to put a smile on the wearer's face.

Celluloid was invented by John Wesley Hyatt in 1869. Celluloid is an artificial, semi-synthetic thermoplastic made from pyroxylin and camphor that resembles ivory. The problem with this early form of celluloid was that it was highly flammable. In 1927, the compound was refined and vinegar was substituted for nitric acid and camphor, so that the material would not be flammable. Decomposition can be detected by examining a piece. Cracks, disintegration, and crystallization are all signs of decomposition. When a piece of celluloid decomposes, it should not be stored with or near other pieces as the decomposition can spread to the other pieces.

In 1908, Leo H. Baekeland invented a thermoplastic that is commonly known as Bakelite. Other names used for this material are catalin, marbelite, durez, and prystal. Bakelite was a cheap and colorful material that was used to make jewelry of all kinds: bangles, brooches, necklaces, rings, and earrings. The material was cast, carved, or laminated into floral and geometric designs and whimsical figurals in the shapes of animals, fruits, hats, fish, and people. Often the jewelry was accented with rhinestones and metal. The material was also hand painted or reverse carved, a method where the Bakelite is carved from the inside so that the design shows on the outside.

Left: charm bracelet with wood notebook charm and wood pencil charm, c. 1940s, $80; middle: heart-shaped brooch with Scottie dog, c. 1940s, $65; right: plastic kiss timer brooch, c. 1940s, $85.

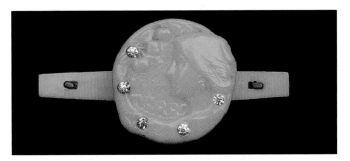

Art Nouveau celluloid brooch with rhinestones, c. 1900, $165.

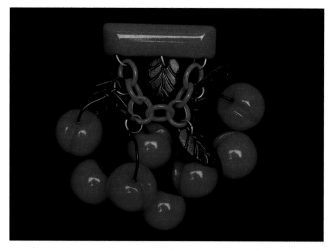

*Brooch with carved Bakelite cherries, c. 1935-1945, **$750**.*

Bakelite can be distinguished from other plastics, because it is heavier than plastic. It will also have a clunking noise when tapped rather than the lightweight clinking sound of plastic. Bakelite will not have any seams in it. A common test for Bakelite is the smell test. You can run a piece under hot water, or rub it, so that the piece gets hot. Then you can smell it. If it smells like carbolic acid then it is Bakelite. Be sure to be careful not to get any accents such as rhinestones, string, or metal on the piece wet when you do this test.

In 1937, Dupont introduced a material known as Lucite. Lucite is a clear material, but is often tinted to add color. Designers used Lucite on its own for jewelry as well as combining it with wood, leather, ceramic, rhinestones, and metals. It became extremely popular for use in jelly bellies where the Lucite is cut into cabochons, and used as the predominate feature of the fish, spiders, elephants, bees, and other creatures.

Due to wartime shortages wood and ceramic were popular materials for designers in the 1940s to create whimsical, novelty jewelry. Sometimes, these materials were used alone while at other times they were combined with Bakelite, Lucite, plastic and metals to create animals, people, florals, Asian, African faces, and other figurals.

*Coro fish Duette with clear and blue rhinestones, **$425**, and Trifari big brooch with clear rhinestones, **$395**.*

$\mathscr{S}ilver$

$\mathscr{S}ilver$ has been a popular material used by designers throughout history. $\mathscr{M}exican$ jewelry and $\mathscr{S}candinavian$ jewelry use silver as their primary metal.

Mexican Silver: 1930-1970

Mexican silversmiths made jewelry for the tourists. The jewelry had pre-Hispanic and traditional Mexican motifs as well as some abstract modern designs. Artisans used silver, a combination of silver with brass or copper, alpaca, amethysts, malachite, obsidian, sodalite, tiger's eye, turquoise, abalone, ebony, rosewood, and enameling to create their original designs.

While hundreds of artists set up their shops in the town of Taxco, Mexico in the 1930s and 1940s, there are only a relatively small number of well-known artisans who gained their reputation for their designs and craftsmanship. William Spratling opened the first workshop in 1929. His early designs were based on traditional Mexican designs. By 1940, he had over 300 artists creating designs for him, which had now become a blend of ancient and modern designs. Many of the well-known designers got their start working for Spratling as apprentices.

Some of the more collectible artists are:

Los Castillo: Brothers Pedro and Carlos Castillo opened their workshop in the 1950s. They used silver as well as inlaid stone and metales casado, which is combining two metals in a piece. Their jewelry is signed Los Castillos.

Antonio Pineda: Used silver with gemstones such as moonstones, topaz, and chrysocolla to create his simple designs that incorporated pre-Hispanic motifs with a modern twist.

Margot de Taxco: Margot van Voohries Carr was married to Antonio Castillo. After her divorce from Antonio, she opened her shop in 1948. She is known for her designs, which incorporate silver and enamel. Her jewelry is signed Margot de Taxco.

Sterling and enamel necklace, earrings, and brooch set, Margot de Taxco, c. 1950s, $1500.

Matilde Eugenia Poulat: Began making jewelry in the 1930s, and in 1950, opened her own shop in Mexico City. She used repousse silver with turquoise, coral, and amethyst to create figurals, pre-Hispanic motifs and crosses. Her jewelry is signed Matl.

Enrique Ledesma: Worked for Spratling and Los Castillo. He opened his shop in 1950. He used inlaid stone as well as plain silver to create his modernistic designs. His jewelry is signed Ledesma with the "L" extending under the signature.

Among the others to look for are: Hector Aguilar, Felipe Martinez, Salvadore Teran, Sigi, Hubert Harmon, Bernice Goodspeed, Los Ballesteros, and Frederick Davis.

Scandinavian Silver: 1900-1960

Scandinavian jewelry consists of jewelry manufactured in Denmark, Norway, Finland, and Sweden. The jewelry has a distinct look and is often identified by its use of flowers, foliates, animal, modern, abstract, and filigree designs. The materials used included silver, bronze, gold, amber, amethyst, chrysoprase, citrine, crystal, lapis, and enamel. The jewelry was generally produced in artist's studios and workshops, where the focus was on design and craftsmanship. Import of the jewelry was relatively small with the large manufacturers being the exception.

Denmark

Georg Jensen of Denmark is a company that is well recognized among collectors. The company is known for its originality of design and quality of craftsmanship. The company began in 1904, and made jewelry and silverware. The earliest designs could be characterized as Art Nouveau and Arts & Crafts. In 1924, Frederick Lunning opened a shop in New York City for Jensen. However, with the advent of World War II, inventory was cut off from Europe, and he had to employ American designers to produce the jewelry. This jewelry was marked Georg Jensen, U.S.A. This jewelry is not as valuable to collectors as the jewelry produced in Denmark by Jensen.

Another noted designer is NE From. From opened his shop in 1931, primarily as a repair shop. By the late 1940s, he was producing his modern designs made of silver and stones that he later exported to the United States in the 1950s and 1960s.

Other Danish designers to look for include Hans Hansen, Henning Koppel, Sigvard Bernadette, and JØrgen Jensen.

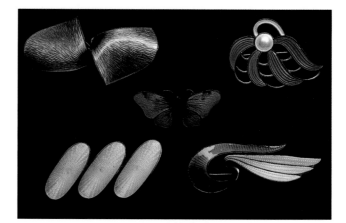

Top left: sterling and enamel leaf brooch, Norway, c. 1950s, $85; top right: sterling with blue and white enamel brooch, maker's mark for Aksel Holmsen, Norway, c. 1950s, $65; middle: sterling and enamel butterfly brooch, Norway, c.1950s, $85; bottom left: sterling and enamel brooch, maker's mark for David Anderson, Norway, c. 1950s, $85; bottom right: sterling with white and green enamel brooch, maker's mark for Aksel Holmsen, Norway, c. 1950s, $95.

Sterling pendant with blue glass, signed NE From, Denmark, c. 1950s, $495.

Norway

In Norway, the traditional Norwegian jewelry is known as sØlje. This type of jewelry is of filigree design with dangling concave disks. Enameling is commonly used on Norwegian jewelry. Marius Hammer was a late nineteenth-century designer who used both the basse-taille and plique-à-jour methods of enameling on silver.

Sterling sØljes earrings, Norway, c. 1950s, $65.

In 1876, David Anderson opened a hollowware and flatware shop. In the early 1900s, he began designing jewelry for his shop. Many of his designs incorporate enameling on silver in both modern and figural designs such as owls, birds, fish, animals, and leaves. His jewelry was exported to the United States after World War II making it more accessible for the collector than some of the other Norwegian designers. Much of his jewelry is signed David-Anderson or D-A, along with the company logo, which is a pair of scales.

Sweden

Swedish designed pieces are not that prevalent and little is known about the designers. Two designers worth noting are Wiwen Nilsson who, after working for Georg Jensen, opened a shop in 1927 to showcase his modern designs, and Sigurd Persson, who is known for his imaginative and original modern designs.

Finland

Pre-World War II jewelry tended to be traditional designs that were influenced by history and cultural motifs. As time progressed, the designs became more creative and inventive. The jewelry evolved into more modern designs. The artists often used silver embellished with the native stones of Finland such as quartz, garnets, and spectrolite. Some designers and companies to note are Elis Kauppi, Kaunis Koru, Lapponia, Kaija Aarikka, and Björn Weckström.

Sterling pendant on black cord, designed by Björn Weckström, Finland, c. 1960s, $900.

*R*hinestones

The History of Rhinestones

Czechoslovakian or Bohemian glass as it was originally known had its beginnings in the 13th and 14th centuries in Bohemia, a part of the Czech Republic. The country has a history rich in glass making including hand blown, molded and cut glass. The introduction of lead compounds is responsible for the clarity and brilliance of the glass, known as lead crystal. The Czechoslovakian glass industry began making rhinestones that were incorporated in their jewelry designs.

Another region responsible for the creation of the rhinestone was Tyrol, Austria. In 1891, Daniel Swarovski revolutionized the jewelry business when he created a new glass-cutting machine that could mechanically cut faceted glass. Previously, it would take long periods of time to finish the stones by hand. Now, the stones could be created in a fraction of the time. Swarovski had a background in glassmaking and he soon began making rhinestones with a 32-percent high lead content that produced faceted stones with refractions unrivaled by any other companies. He also innovated the rhinestone business by creating vacuum plating for the backs of the stones with silver and gold. By doing this, he again reduced the need for hand labor. Through all of his efforts, ingenuity, and imagination, today Swarovski stones are thought of as the highest-quality rhinestones, and are used by over 85 percent of the American jewelry companies. The company is now located in Providence, Rhode Island.

The term rhinestone came from the Rhine River in Austria. The river in the late 1800s was filled with quartz pebbles in brilliant colors. As this source was depleted, imitation glass rhinestones replaced them. Rhinestones are highly reflective glass made to

Brooch and matching earrings with lavender, hot pink, and purple rhinestones, $185.

imitate gems. They are molded, leaded glass of all colors. A rhinestone is always backed with a thin metallic layer of gold or silver to bounce the light off of the glass for brilliancy and to create their sparkling quality.

Just as rhinestones were created as imitations of real gems, the rhinestone was also being imitated. "Stones" made of plastic were being offered in a myriad of colors as an even less-expensive alternative to the glass stones.

Cuts and Shapes

Rhinestones are both affordable and fashionable. They come in many shapes and sizes. The various cuts are:

Baguette: A narrow, elongated, rectangular-shaped, faceted stone.

Cabochon: A round dome-shaped stone with a flat back, usually opaque or translucent, but can be a foiled back.

Chaton: A stone that has eight facets on top and eight facets on the bottom. The top is flat and the bottom comes to a point. There are several parts of a chaton. The flat top is known as a table. The girdle is the place where the top and the bottom of the stone meet. The crown is the part of the stone that is above the girdle. The pavilion is the bottom part of the stone under the girdle. The culet is the point of the stone.

Dentelles: A stone that is formed in a mold and then hand cut. There are either 18, 32, or 64 facets on the back and front of the stone. Light is refracted through the facets in the stone's surface.

Unfoiled dentelles: This stone was popular in the 1920s through the 1940s. It is a large glass stone that is molded and then hand cut to add facets. The light is refracted through the faceted cuts on the glass.

Emerald Cut: A rectangular cut stone with faceted edges.

Flat Back Rhinestone: The stone's top is faceted and its back is flat.

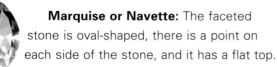

Marquise or Navette: The faceted stone is oval-shaped, there is a point on each side of the stone, and it has a flat top.

Mine Cut: A square stone with rounded corners, sometimes called a cushion shape. Thirty-two crown facets and 24 pavilion facets with a table and a culet.

Pear Cut: A faceted teardrop-shaped stone.

Princess Cut: A faceted, square-cut stone, sometimes now known as a quadrillium or squarillion cut.

Rose Cut: A flat-base stone with 24 triangular facets meeting at the top with a point.

Round Cut: See flat back rhinestone.

Square Octagon Cut: A square cut stone with faceted edges.

Tapered Baguette: A narrow, elongated, rectangular-shaped, faceted stone that is largest at one end and then slims down toward the other end.

Triangle Cut: A triangular-cut, faceted stone based on a brilliant-style cut.

Note: A mine cut, princess cut, and rose cut are types of cuts that are generally used for real gemstones, though some have been used for gemstones such as garnets, and on very rare occasions for rhinestones. I've included them above because the terms are often bandied about, but collectors should be aware that these cuts are rarely used for rhinestones.

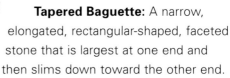

Settings

Several different types of settings are used for rhinestones.

Bead Set: Small burrs of metal rise out of the pin's base to hold the individual rhinestones in place.

A bead setting.

Handset: Stones are glued in individually in a scooped-out cup in the metal.

A bead setting.

Bezel Set: A way of setting the stone in which the stone is held in place by a band of metal that is placed around the outside of each stone. This method is both time consuming and expensive.

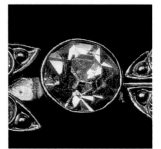

A bezel setting.

Handset with Metal Prongs: Stones are handset and then the metal prongs are bent over the stone's top.

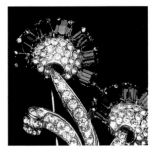

A handset with metal prongs.

Channel Set: Occurs when the rhinestones rest in a metal channel and are held in only by a slight rim that runs along the edge of the channel. In this method, the stones are set side-by-side so no metal is seen between the stones.

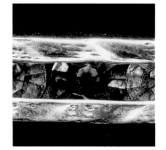

A channel setting.

Pave Set: Occurs when the stones are set together in a group so that the underlying metal surface is hidden.

A pave setting.

Prong Set: Stones are set and then metal prongs are bent over the stone's top by a machine.

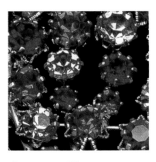

A prong setting.

Metals and Other Materials

There are many types of materials used in the creation of costume jewelry.

Bakelite: A thermo plastic material invented in 1909.

Base Metal: Non-precious metals which include zinc, tin, and lead.

Celluloid: Invented in 1868, this is a lightweight, semi-synthetic, part cellulose, natural-cotton fiber that resembles plastic.

Coin Silver: A mixture of 90% silver and 10% other metal. It is the standard content of silver coins.

French Jet: Black glass.

German Silver: A mixture of nickel, copper, and zinc. It is also known as nickel silver or gunmetal.

Gold: In the United States, the purity of gold is designated by karat. Pure gold is 24k, but is often too soft. Copper, silver, zinc, and nickel are added to strengthen the gold. The amount added determines the karat of the gold. In Europe, the purity of gold is designated by fineness. Pure gold is 1000 fine.

Gold Filled: Made by joining a layer of gold to base metal. It is not filled with gold, and it is thicker and more durable than rolled gold plate.

Gold Plating: Plating is used to give the appearance of gold. White metal is dipped into a copper bath, and then dipped into a nickel or chromium bath.

Electromagnetic acid is added so that the gold plating will adhere to the metal.

Gutta-percha: A hardened tree rubber.

Hard Gold Electroplated: An electrical process is used to apply a thin coating of gold to base metal.

Japanned Metal: Metal that is coated with a coal tar derivative to give it a black color.

Jet: A lightweight fossilized coal.

Lucite: Thermoplastic, Dupont trade name.

Nickel Silver: A white metal mixture of copper, zinc, and nickel.

Pewter: A lead alloy.

Plastic: A lightweight, synthetic material.

Pot Metal: A mixture of metals that were all thrown into a pot and melted down. This type of metal was prevalent and is recognizable due to its dull finish.

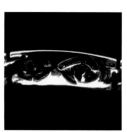

Rhodium: A non-tarnishing white metal that resembles platinum. It has a shiny, bright veneer. It is an expensive finish, and is often used to plate base metals to give them a platinum-like sheen.

Rolled Gold Plate: A layer of gold alloy is applied to a layer of base metal, and then drawn to the thickness needed.

Silver Plate: Electricity is used to apply a coating of silver to base metal.

Sterling: A silver compound that contains 92.5% silver. Sterling silver will usually be hallmarked with the word "sterling," or an assay mark on the piece's back. This was widely used during World War II, because the other metals that had traditionally been used in jewelry production were being used for the war effort.

Sterling Vermeil: Sterling silver that is dipped in a gold plating, generally yellow or rose gold.

Vulcanite: A hardened rubber.

White Metal: A mixture of 92% tin with cadmium, lead, and zinc.

Collecting Costume Jewelry

The first rule of collecting is to collect what you like! Don't worry about trends or what's the hot new collectible. Focus on amassing a collection that makes you smile, intrigues you, and inspires you. Let your imagination run wild. The possibilities are endless. A collection can consist of bird pins, bracelets, or jewelry made by a particular designer or design style. After that, focus on condition and quality. Is the piece well made? Is it missing any stones or pieces? Can the piece be repaired, and how much will the repair cost? These are all questions that you need to ask yourself when you are purchasing a piece of jewelry. But remember to enjoy yourself. Part of the fun is the thrill of the hunt, and finding that one piece that makes your heart stop!

Helpful Hints

• Be conscious of the piece's condition, because it will affect its value. If the stones are yellowed, dark, or missing, the value and the price should not be comparable to pieces that are in excellent to mint condition.

• Unless a piece is rare, or one that you truly desire, think twice before purchasing an item that is not in good condition. However, if you are able to repair the piece yourself or through a jeweler, and the price is reflective of the condition, then it might be worthwhile to purchase.

• To be considered in excellent condition, the piece should have all of the stones and component parts, e.g., no missing or broken clasps, settings, or findings.

• Often, there is leeway in terms of condition when it comes to enameling. Over the years, enameling will become a bit worn. This means slight age wear, not chips and severe wear.

• Don't be talked into buying a piece simply because it is signed. Just because a piece of jewelry is signed, does not mean that it is more valuable. This is a myth that seems to be continually perpetuated. There are many pieces in the market that are unsigned, and just as valuable as signed pieces. At the same time, there are signed pieces that have little value at all. So do not base your purchase merely on the fact that it is signed.

• Do not accept excuses for low-quality jewelry. I have often heard dealers tell customers that missing stones, yellowed stones, and broken pieces are acceptable because that is a sign of age. This is a sign of damage and you should not be talked into accepting damaged goods based upon this excuse.

• Be aware that when a piece of jewelry is a popular item, the price may be artificially high and have no bearing on the intrinsic value.

• Take your time to examine the piece. Use a loupe to look for signatures and other marks as well as damage.

$\mathcal{P}$rice Guide

The following is a price guide featuring hundreds of examples of jewelry from the 1800s through the 1990s. The values in the price guide are only a reference point. Values vary according to each piece's condition, quality, design, and/or geographic location where the piece is purchased.

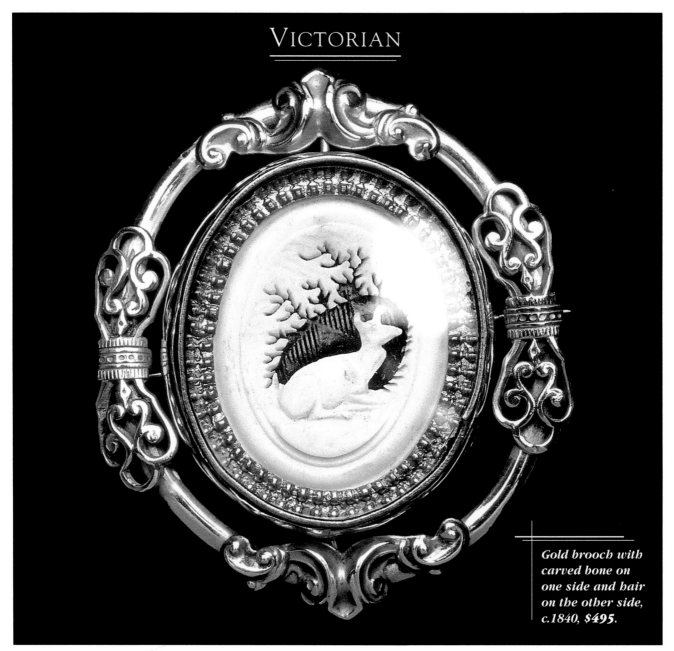

VICTORIAN

Gold brooch with carved bone on one side and hair on the other side, c.1840, $495.

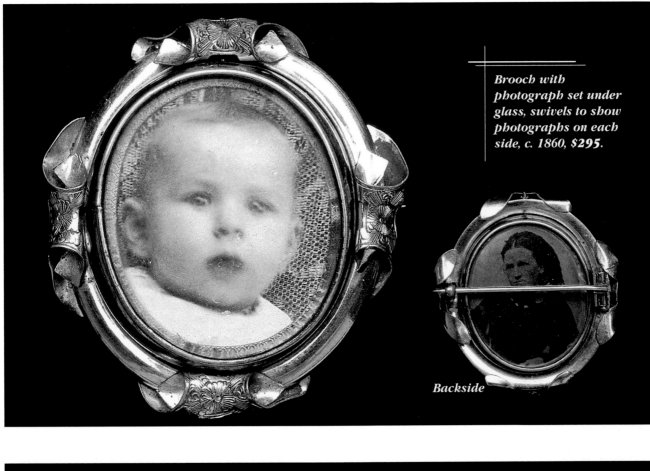

Brooch with photograph set under glass, swivels to show photographs on each side, c. 1860, $295.

Backside

Hardstone cameo brooch, c. 1900, $475.

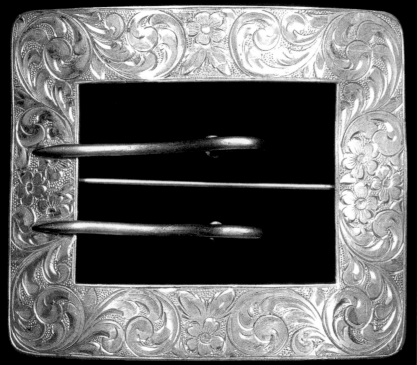

Sterling buckle sash pin, c. 1880, $195.

Gold brooch, Prince of Wales plumes of hair with seed pearls, c.1840, $1850.

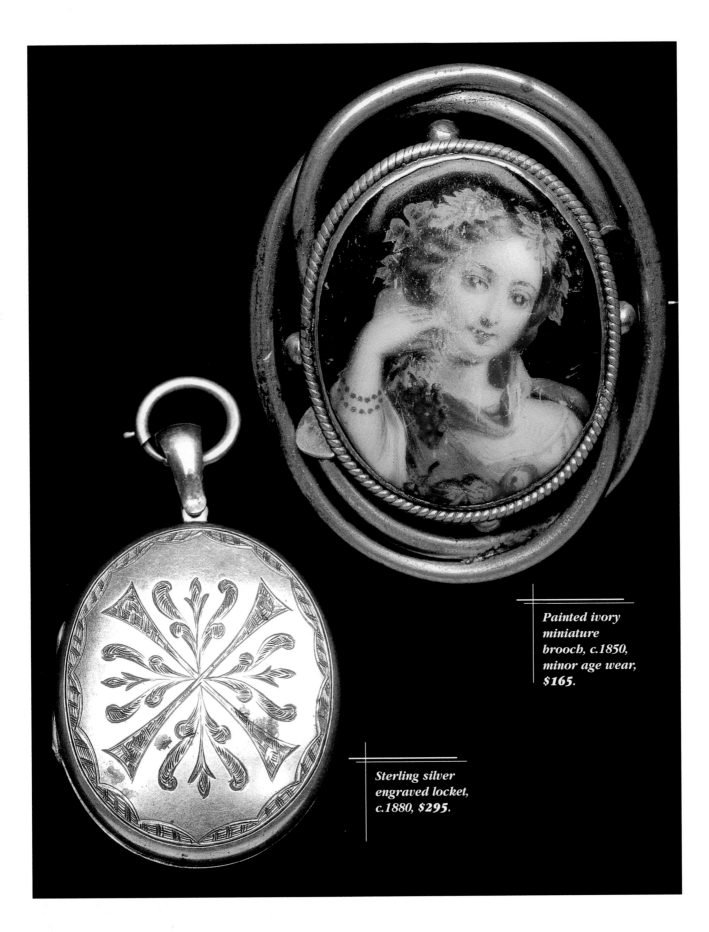

Painted ivory miniature brooch, c.1850, minor age wear, $165.

Sterling silver engraved locket, c.1880, $295.

Locket on chain with seed pearls, c.1880, $225.

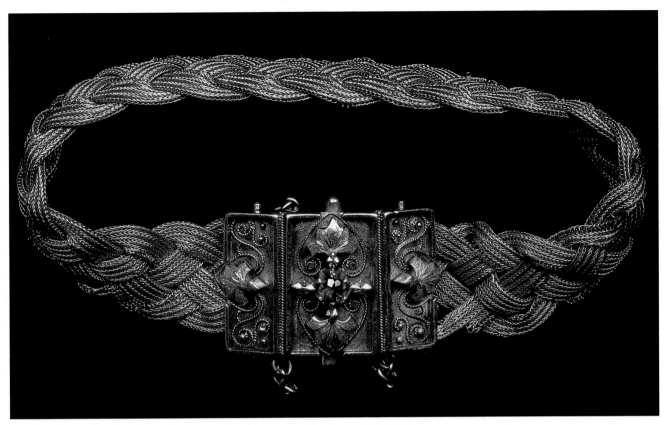

*14k gold bracelet with ruby, minor damage to the gold braid, c. 1850, **$795**.*

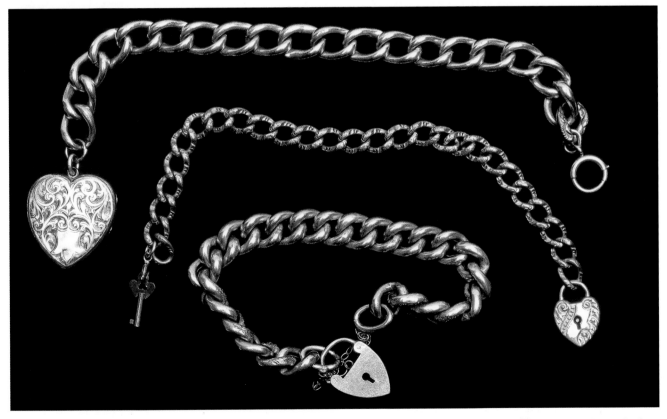

*Top: link bracelet with heart charm, c. 1890, **$295**; middle: heart lock bracelet with key, c.1890, **$250**; bottom: heart lock bracelet, c.1890, **$250**.*

Locket on chain with seed pearls, gold filled, c. 1900, $525.

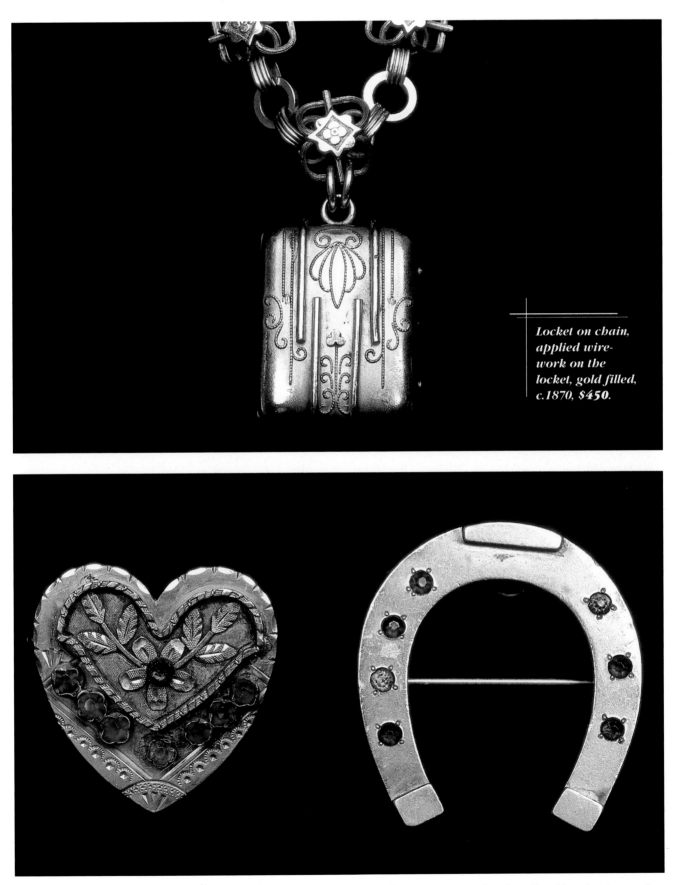

Locket on chain, applied wire-work on the locket, gold filled, c.1870, $450.

Left: heart-shaped pin with red, green and topaz glass stones, c. 1890, $110; right: horseshoe brooch with red, green and topaz glass stones, c. 1880, $145.

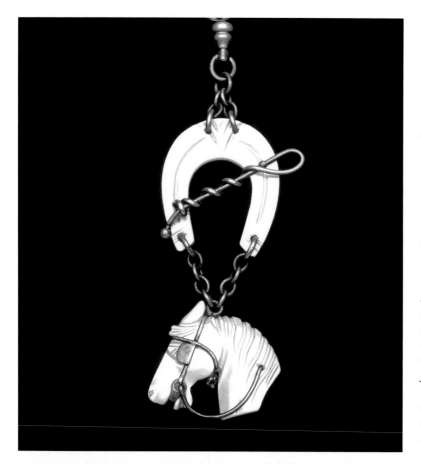

Necklace with mother-of-pearl horse and horseshoe pendant, c.1900, **$325**.

Top left: brooch with photograph, c.1900, **$95**; top middle: brooch with photograph under glass with engraved gold frame, c.1890, **$245**; top right: brooch with photograph of two children with blue enameling, some wear to the enameling, c.1880, **$90**; bottom left: brooch with photograph of two children, floral design frame with white and blue enameling, c.1880, **$110**; bottom middle: brooch with photograph under glass, c.1880, **$85**; bottom right: brooch with photograph under glass with gold rope frame, c.1860, **$145**.

Top: Etruscan revival locket with turquoise, c. 1870, $145; bottom: Etruscan revival bar pin with amethyst, c. 1860, $155.

*Left: shell cameo brooch with enameled frame, c. 1870, **$165**; right: shell cameo brooch, c. 1860, **$375**.*

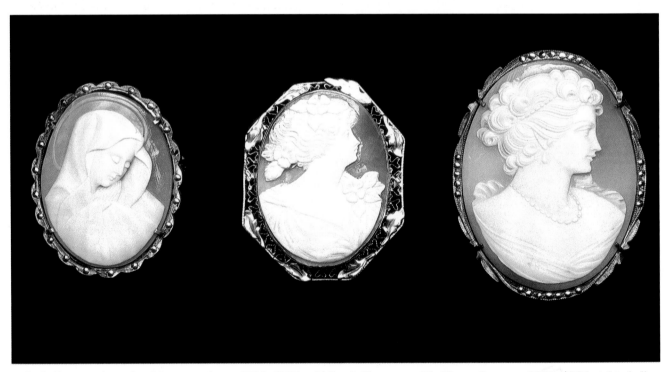

*Left: shell cameo brooch with marcasites, c.1900, **$325**; middle: shell cameo with filigree frame, c. 1920, **$225**; right: shell cameo with sterling silver frame with marcasites, c. 1920, **$395**.*

*Top left: yellow gold brooch with seed pearls and diamond, c.1860, **$195**; top right: brooch with taille d'épargne, yellow gold, c. 1870, **$145**; bottom left: brooch with taille d'épargne, yellow gold, c. 1870, **$165**; bottom right: brooch with taille d'épargne and coral, yellow gold, c. 1870, **$110**.*

*Top left: double heart sterling silver pin, c.1887, **$165**; top right: sterling silver engraved brooch with hair compartment on the back, c.1885, **$145**; middle: sterling brooch with engraved "Clara", c. 1880, **$95**; bottom left: sterling silver Mizpah pin, c.1880, **$110**; bottom right: sterling pin with heart and anchors, c.1887, **$115**.*

Sterling bookchain necklace with onyx, seed pearl, and marcasite pendant, c. 1870, $395.

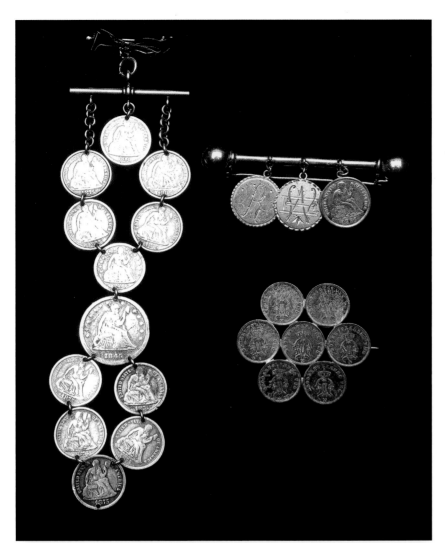

Left: brooch with coin love tokens, bow later addition, c.1880, one side engraved with names, $375; top right: sterling brooch with coin love tokens, c.1890, $275; bottom right: silver brooch with coin love tokens, c.1890, $125.

Gold-filled link bracelet with gold charms accented with mother-of-pearl, turquoise, rubies, and glass stones, c.1890, $850.

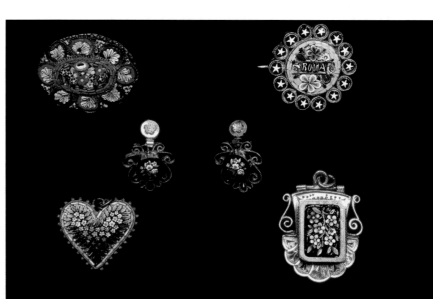

*Top left: micromosaic brooch with floral design, c.1900, **$125**; top right: micromosaic brooch, c. 1880, **$225**; middle: gold-filled earrings with micromosaics, c.1870, **$195**; bottom left: heart-shaped micromosaic pendant, c.1880, **$450**; bottom right: gold-filled micromosaic watch fob, c.1890, **$395**.*

*Cut steel buckles, c. 1850-1900, left: **$85**; top middle: **$35**; middle: **$45**; bottom middle: **$45**; right: **$85**.*

*Top left: gold-filled pin with red glass stone, c.1880, **$110**; middle left: gold-filled pin with opal and blue glass stone, c.1860, **$125**; bottom left: 10k pin with seed pearls and pink glass stone, c.1860, small crack in the pin, **$125**; top right: gold-filled pin with coral, c.1890, **$145**; bottom right: gold-filled pin, c.1890, **$110**.*

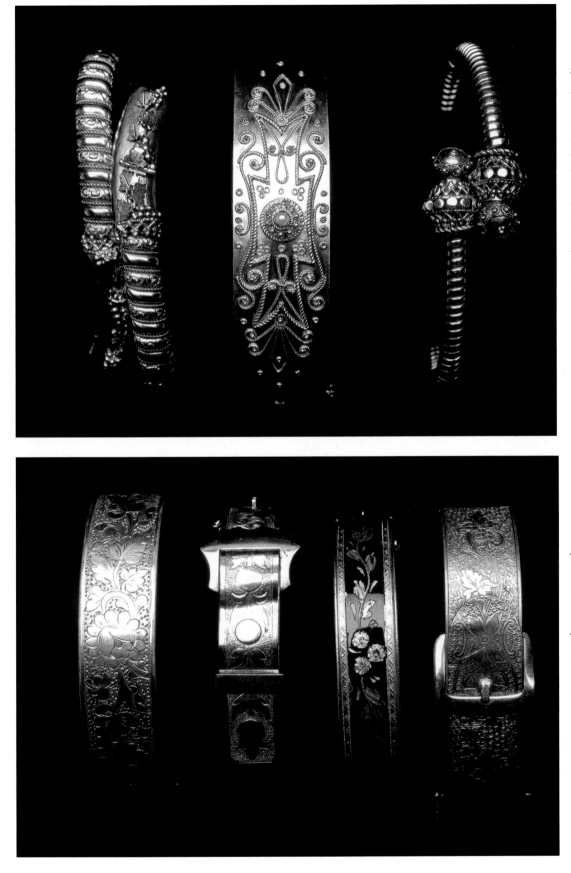

Left: gold-filled wraparound bracelet with applied leaves and beads, c.1890, **$185**; middle: gold-filled hinged bangle with applied wirework and seed pearl, c.1880, **$495**; right: gold-filled wraparound bracelet, c.1890, **$185**.

Left to right: gold-filled hinged ban-gle, c.1900, **$175**; gold-filled hinged buckle bangle, c. 1890, **$145**; gold-filled hinged taille d'épargne bangle, c.1870, **$185**; gold-filled engraved hinged bangle, c.1900, **$145**.

*Gunmetal pendant
on long-chain with
faceted glass,
c.1900, $495.*

Left: gold-filled earrings, c.1840, $165; right: gold-filled earrings with seed pearls, c.1840, $145.

Black enameled ring with glass compartment containing braided hair, c.1830, $345.

Mosaic earrings, c.1880, $350.

Gold-filled necklace with ruby cabochons, c. 1870, $295.

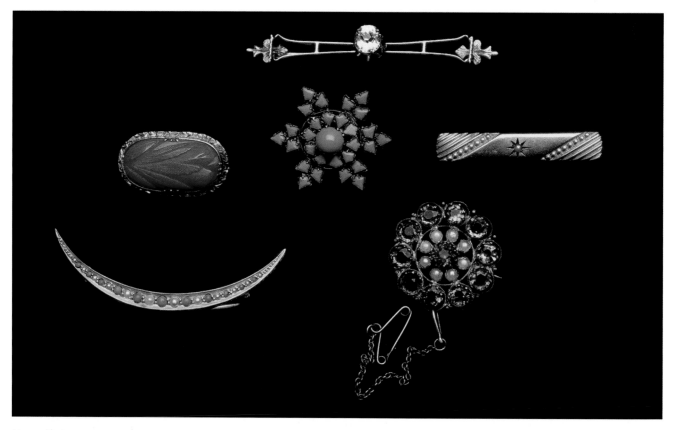

*Top: 14k bar pin with faceted glass, c. 1900, **$145**; middle left: coral pin in gold-filled frame, c.1850, **$185**; middle: snowflake pin with turquoise, c. 1860, **$90**; middle right: 10k bar pin with seed pearl, c.1860, **$100**; bottom left: 14k crescent moon pin with seed pearls and turquoise, c. 1850, **$155**; bottom right: pin with seed pearls and amethysts, c. 1840, **$265**.*

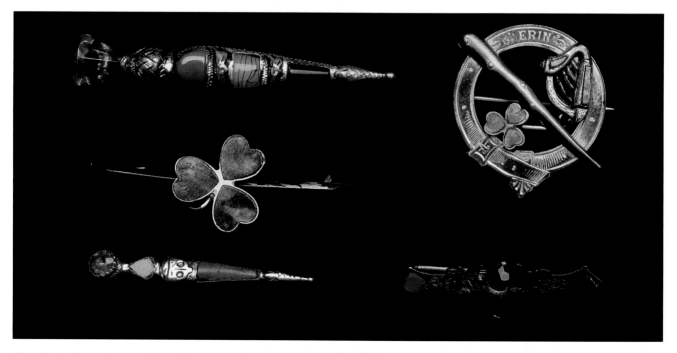

*Top left: sterling claymore pin with agate and cairngorm, c. 1890, **$295**; middle left: sterling shamrock bar pin with green agate, c. 1900, **$95**; bottom left: sterling claymore pin with red agate, opal and citrine glass, c.1890, **$165**; top right: brass pin with green agate, c.1900, **$95**; bottom right: sterling thistle pin with red and green agate and amethyst glass, c. 1900, **$85**.*

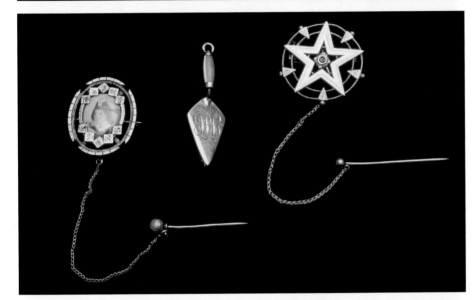

*Left: sterling engraved, hinged bangle, c.1880, **$395**; middle: sterling double bangle with red glass stone, c. 1870, **$145**; right: sterling engraved, hinged bangle, c.1880, **$495**.*

*Left: miniature painted on ivory set in gold-filled engraved frame, c.1850, **$365**; middle: gold-filled engraved trowel pin, c. 1860, **$185**; right: gold-filled star pin with ruby cabachon, c.1860, **$225**.*

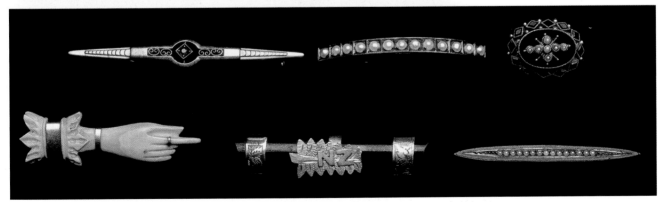

*Top left: gold bar pin with ruby, c. 1900, **$185**; top middle: 14k green gold pin with seed pearls, c. 1840, **$395**; top right: French jet pin with seed pearls, 18k, c. 1850, **$155**; bottom left: ivory hand pin, c. 1850, **$495**; bottom middle: agate bar pin with applied gold-filled bands, c. 1880, **$165**; bottom right: sterling bar pin with enameling and seed pearls, c.1900, **$95**.*

*Whitby jet bead
necklace with
pendant, c.1870,
$850.*

Bog Oak brooch,
*c.1860, **$325**.*

Micromosaic brooch,
black glass with inlaid
*glass, c.1860, **$165**.*

Top left: jet bar pin,
c.1870, $125; top right:
jet bar pin, c. 1860,
$165; bottom: jet
*brooch, c.1860, **$145**.*

*Left: Whitby jet pendant with engraving on the back, c.1870, **$300**; top middle: Whitby jet brooch, c.1870,*
***$195**; bottom middle: Whitby jet brooch with beads, c.1870, **$295**; right: Whitby jet cameo, c.1870, **$495**.*

*Top: black enameled hinged bangle with applied gold-filled leaves and seed pearls, c. 1900, **$265**; bottom: jet pin with gold-filled anchor and seed pearls, c.1850, **$185**.*

*Garnet earrings, c.1900, **$450**.*

Vulcanite cameo pendant on necklace made with jet beads and composite beads, c.1860, $395.

Jet cameo pendant on French jet beads, c.1860, $625.

Garland-style necklace, pot metal and rhinestones, c. 1915, $245.

*Left to right: sterling, filigree, hinged bangle with clear and green glass, c. 1915, **$185**; sterling, filigree, hinged bangle with amethyst glass, c. 1915, **$145**; sterling, filigree, hinged bangle with clear rhinestones and blue glass, c. 1915, **$120**; sterling, filigree, hinged bangle with blue glass, c. 1915, **$110**.*

─────────────

*Sterling necklace with faceted amethyst glass, c. 1910, **$165**.*

Necklace, pot metal and rhinestones, c.1910, $145.

Left: brooch with seed pearls, rhinestones, and amethyst-faceted glass, c. 1900, $245; top right: bar pin with faux pearls and rhinestones, c.1910, $70; bottom right: sterling filigree bar pin, clear rhinestones and green glass, c. 1915, $100.

Festoon-style necklace, sterling with clear rhinestones and faceted glass, c.1900, $495.

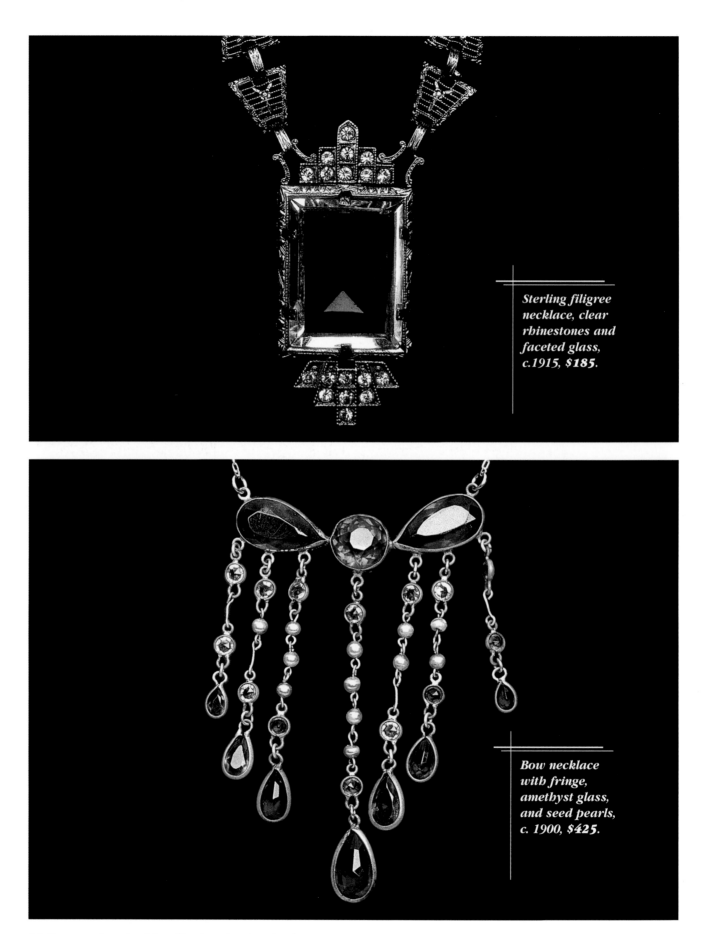

Sterling filigree necklace, clear rhinestones and faceted glass, c.1915, $185.

Bow necklace with fringe, amethyst glass, and seed pearls, c. 1900, $425.

*Sterling filigree
pendant on chain,
clear rhinestones
and blue glass,
c. 1910, $110.*

Gold brooch with amethysts and seed pearls, c. 1905, $1200.

Negligee-style necklace, sterling with blue faceted glass, c. 1900, $155.

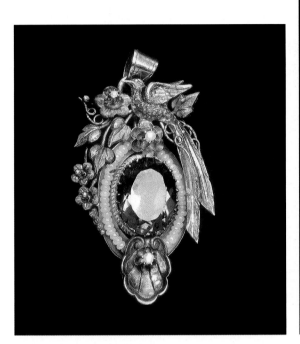

Gold pendant with enameling, seed pearls and amethysts, c. 1900, $850.

Sterling bow pendant on chain, clear rhinestones, c. 1900, $185.

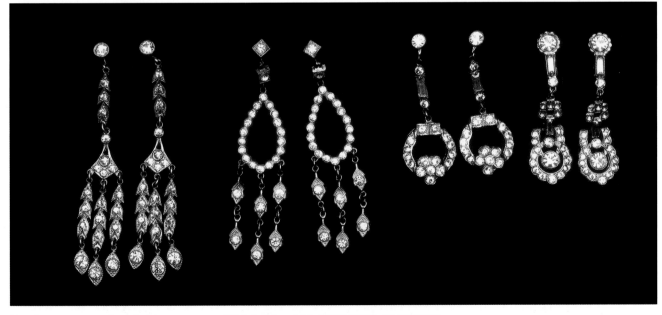

Earrings, pot metal and rhinestones, c. 1910, left to right: $110; $110; $145; $155.

*Sterling pendant
on chain, clear
rhinestones,
c. 1910, $165.*

Sterling pendant on chain with rhinestones and amethyst glass, c. 1910, $285.

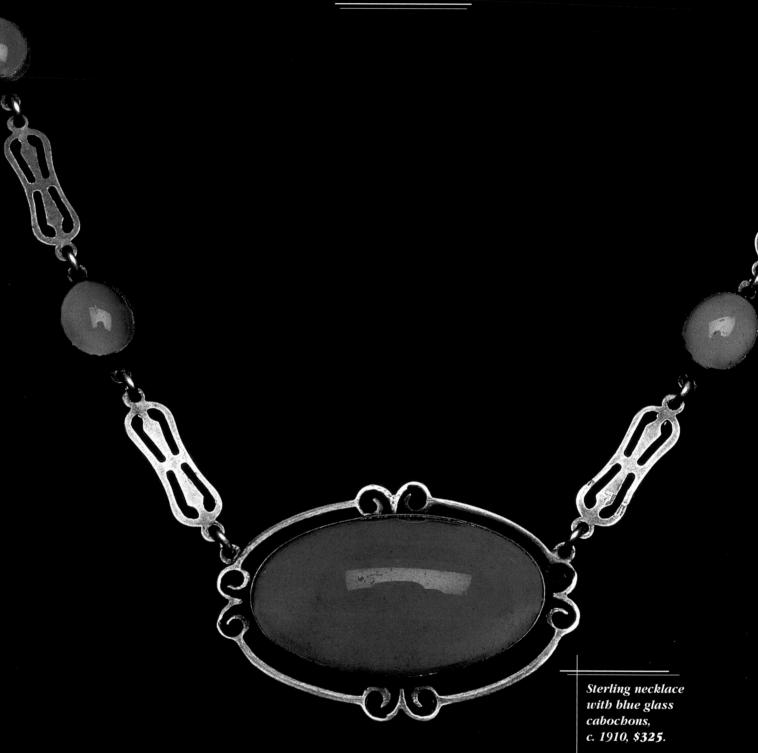

Sterling necklace with blue glass cabochons, c. 1910, $325.

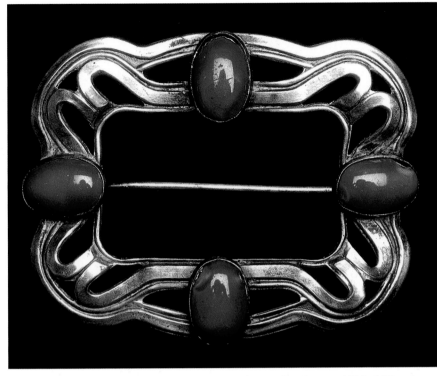

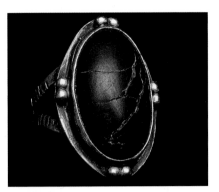

Sterling ring with green turquoise cabochon, c. 1900, $375.

Sterling brooch with agate, c.1900, $225.

Sash ornament/pin with blue glass, some chips to the glass, c. 1900, $95.

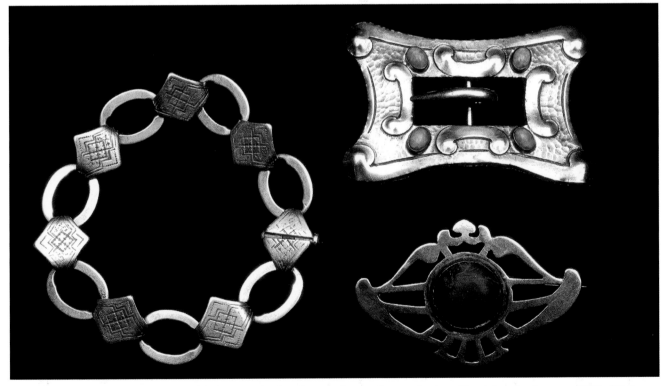

Left: sterling link bracelet, c.1900, $350; top right: hand-wrought, sterling sash pin with pink cabochons, c. 1900, $375; bottom right: sterling brooch with lapis, c. 1900, $350.

*Left: sterling necklace with amethyst glass, c. 1900, $185; top right: Georg Jensen sterling tulip-design pin with cabochon, c. 1930, $400; bottom right: sterling phoenix pin with amethyst, c. 1915, **$425**.*

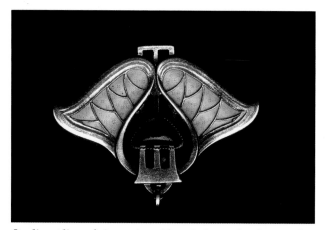

*Sterling plique à jour pin with red glass cabochon and freshwater pearl, c. 1900, **$1600**.*

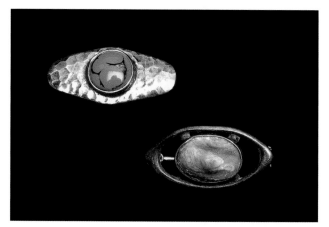

*Top: sterling hand-hammered pin with turquoise, c. 1910, **$125**; bottom: sterling pin with blister pearl, c. 1900, **$80**.*

ART NOUVEAU

Brass pendant on chain, amethyst glass, c. 1905, $155.

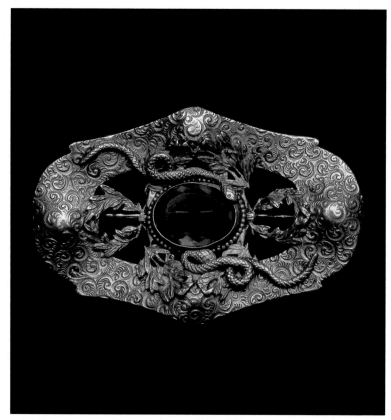

*Brass sash ornament/pin with amethyst glass, c. 1900, **$195**.*

*Brass horse pin with pendant, topaz glass, c. 1905, **$395**.*

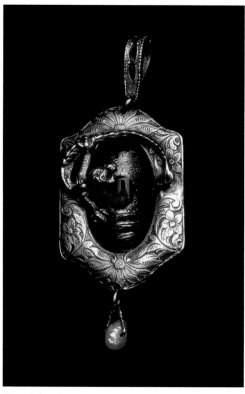

*Brass pendant with green glass bead and freshwater pearl, c. 1900, **$225**.*

*Brass sash ornament/pin with seed pearls and amethyst glass, c. 1900, **$185**.*

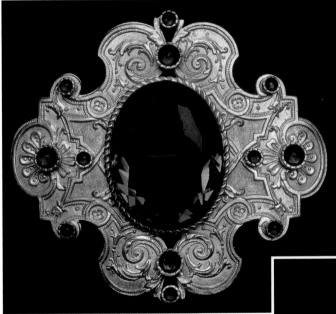

*Sterling Wm. B Kerr brooch,
c. 1900, **$950**.*

*Brass sash ornament/pin with
amethyst glass, c. 1895, **$195**.*

*Silver sash ornament/pin
with rhinestone and coral,
c. 1900, **$150**.*

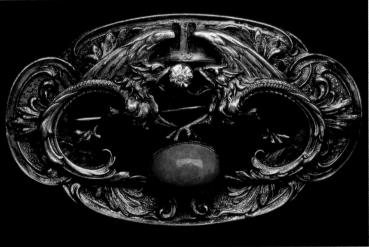

Brass sash ornament/pin with topaz glass and green rhinestones, c. 1895, $195.

Brass earrings, c. 1895, $145.

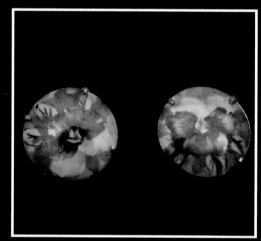

Hand-painted porcelain earrings, c. 1900, $95.

Brass earrings with amethyst glass, c. 1895, $125.

Brass pendant on chain with floral plaques, topaz glass, c. 1900, $395.

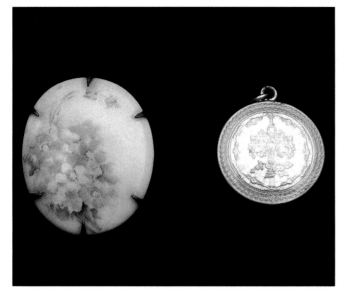

Left: hand-painted porcelain pin, c. 1900, **$85**; *right: enameled locket, c. 1900,* **$195**.

Top: gold-filled locket, c. 1900, **$165**; *bottom left: gold-filled locket with rhinestones, c. 1900,* **$95**; *right: gold-filled locket with rhinestones, c. 1900,* **$125**.

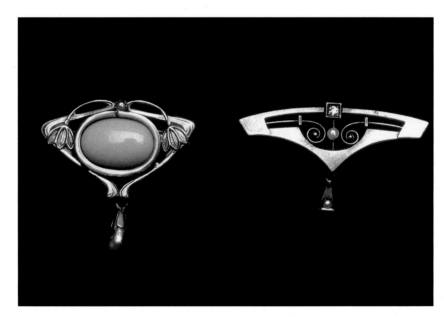

Top: brass pin with citrine, c. 1900, **$185**; *bottom: sterling pin with citrine, c. 1895,* **$110**.

Left: 14k pin with cabachon and pearls, c. 1900, **$650**; *right: 14k pin with diamond and pearl, c.1910,* **$375**.

*Brass sash ornament/pin with rhinestones, c. 1895, **$95** each.*

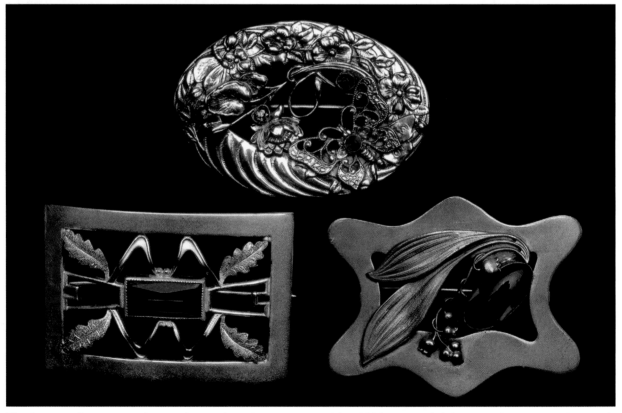

*Top: brass sash ornament/pin with amethyst rhinestones, c. 1900, **$125**; bottom left: brass sash ornament/pin with amethyst glass, c. 1900, **$125**; bottom right: brass sash ornament/pin, c. 1895, **$135**.*

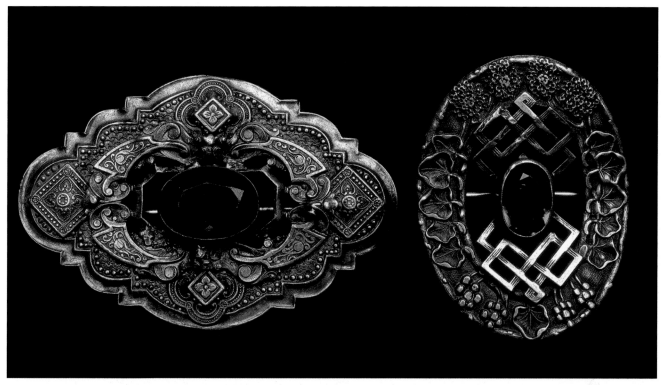

*Left: silver sash ornament/pin with green glass, c. 1895, **$190**; right: silver sash ornament/pin, c. 1895, **$150**.*

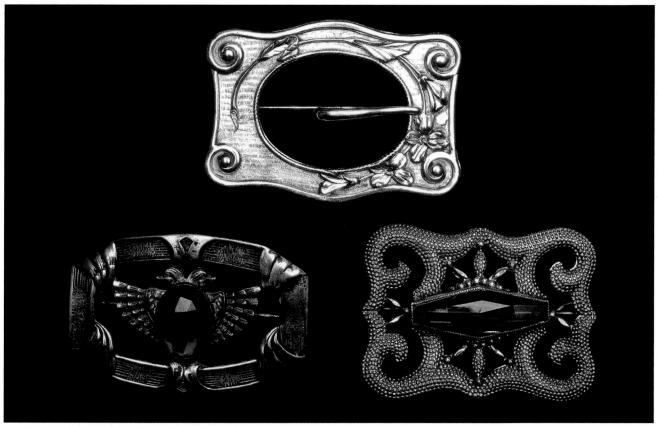

*Top: silver sash ornament/pin, c. 1895, **$75**; bottom left: silver sash ornament/pin with amethyst glass, c. 1900, **$110**; bottom right: silver sash ornament/pin with amethyst glass, c. 1900, **$125**.*

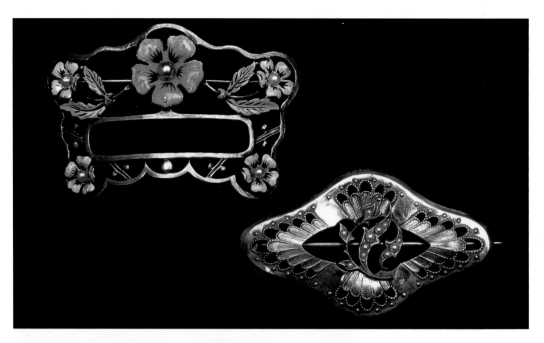

*Top: brass sash ornament/pin with enameling and faux pearls, c. 1895, **$245**; bottom: brass sash ornament/pin with faux pearls, c. 1895, **$145**.*

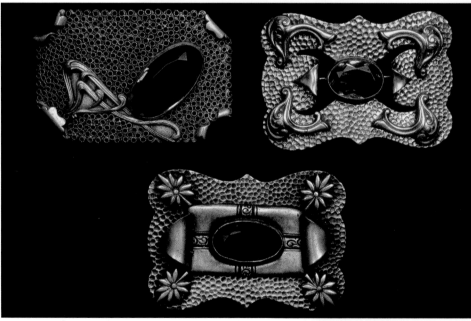

*Top left: brass sash ornament/pin with amethyst glass, c. 1895, **$195**; top right: brass sash ornament/pin with amethyst glass, c. 1895, **$195**; bottom: brass sash ornament/pin with amethyst glass, c. 1895, **$185**.*

*Left: brass sash ornament/pin with green glass, c. 1895, **$110**; right: brass sash ornament/pin with topaz glass, c. 1895, **$145**.*

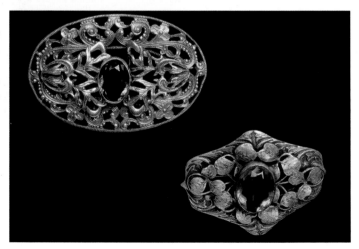

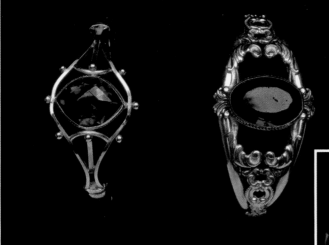

Left: gold-filled hinged bangle with amethyst glass, c. 1910, $165; right: gold-filled hinged bangle with amethyst glass, marked FM Co., c. 1910, $155.

Gold-filled hinged bangle with rhinestones, c. 1900, $195.

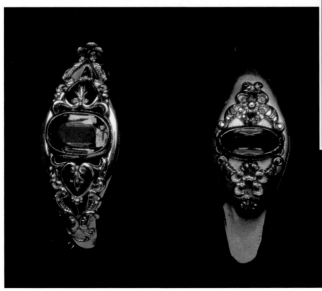

Left: 14k gold lion's head ring with rubies, c. 1900, $300; right: 14k gold ring with floral design work and green turquoise, c. 1900, $425.

Yellow-metal hinged bangle with faceted glass, applied flowers, and leaves, c. 1910, $275.

Left: gold-filled hinged bangle with topaz glass, c. 1910, $155; right: gold-filled hinged bangle with blue glass, marked FM Co., c.1910, $155.

*Top left: brass bar pin with green and pink glass, c. 1900, **$155**; bottom left: brass bar pin with green glass, c. 1900, **$125**; right: brass pin with green glass, c.1900, **$65**.*

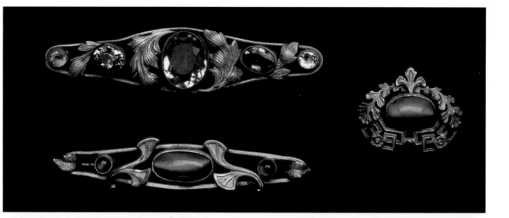

*Top: brass bar pin with blue rhinestones, c. 1910, **$55**; middle: brass bar pin with faux pearls and faux coral, c. 1910, **$60**; bottom: brass bar pin with glass and rhinestones, c. 1910, **$85**.*

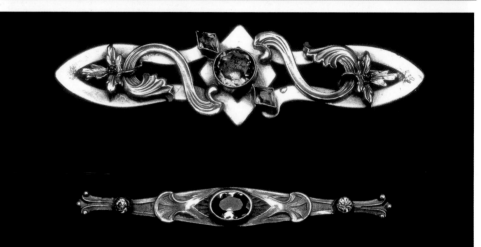

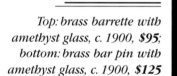

*Top: brass barrette with amethyst glass, c. 1900, **$95**; bottom: brass bar pin with amethyst glass, c. 1900, **$125***

*Top left: silver bar pin, c. 1900, **$95**; bottom left: brass dragonfly pin with green and red rhinestones, c. 1900, **$130**; right: sterling engraved floral pin, c. 1905, **$35**.*

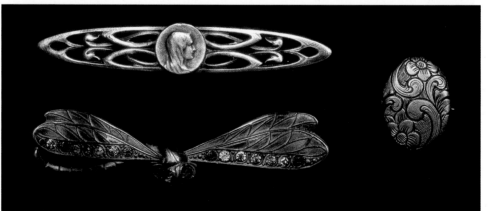

1920s & 1930s

Czechoslovakian necklace, brass, enameling, topaz rhinestones, and amethyst glass, c.1925, $795.

*Left: Art Deco brooch with rhinestones and amethyst glass, c. 1930, **$165**; right: grape design dress clip with faux pearls and rhinestones, c. 1930, **$100**.*

*Left: pot metal bird brooch with rhine-stones, c. 1920, **$245**; right: sterling bird brooch with green glass and rhine-stones, c. 1930, **$255**.*

*Top: 14k brooch with rose quartz, jade and diamonds, c. 1925, **$600**; bottom: Czechoslovakian brooch with green glass and rhinestones, c. 1930, **$225**.*

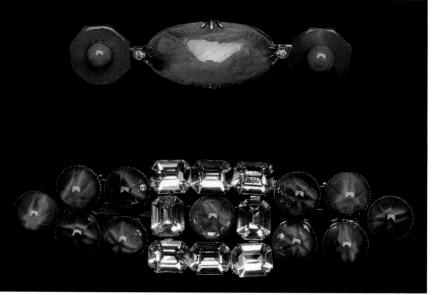

Art Deco Coro Duettes, c. 1935; top left: $175; bottom left: $195; top right: $185; bottom right: $165.

Left: Art Deco dress clips, pot metal with rhinestones, c. 1925, $145; right: floral dress clips, pot metal and rhinestones, c. 1925, $165.

Pot metal and rhinestone necklace, c. 1920, $195.

*Art Deco floral design
brooch, rhodium,
and rhinestones, c.
1920, $495.*

*Art Deco brooch, pot
metal, rhinestones,
and faux pearls, c.
1920, $145.*

*Bow brooch, pot metal
with blue and clear
rhinestones, c. 1925, $165.*

*Art Deco brooch, pot
metal, and rhinestones,
c. 1925, $185.*

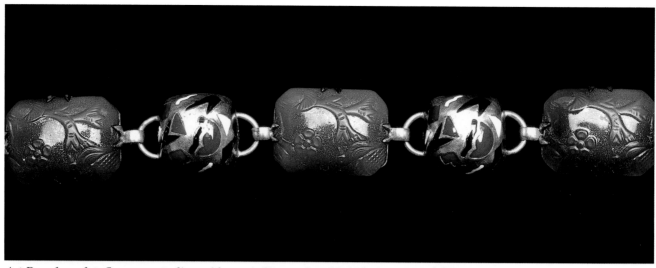

*Art Deco bracelet, Germany, sterling with enameling and molded glass, c. 1920, **$650**.*

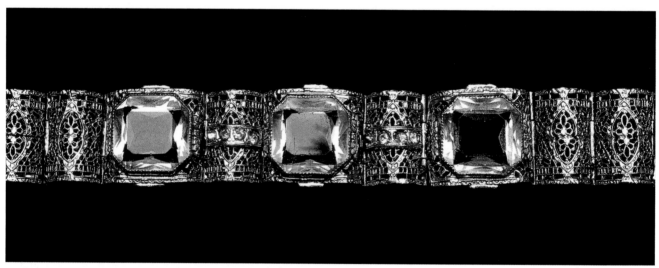

*Sterling filigree bracelet with blue glass, c. 1920, **$385**.*

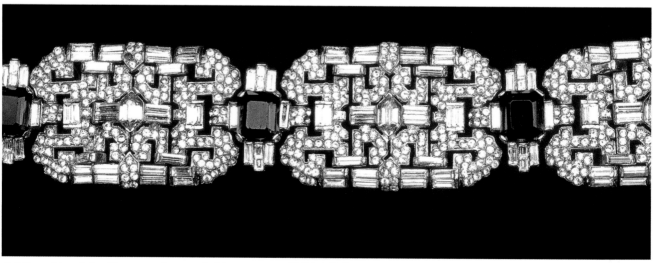

*Art Deco bracelet with green glass and rhinestones, c. 1925, **$495**.*

Butterfly brooches with rhinestones and glass, c. 1925, $285 each.

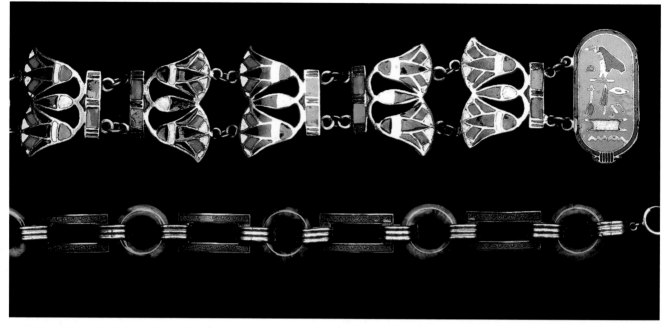

Top: Egyptian revival bracelet, sterling with enameling, c. 1925, $425; bottom: Art Deco slave bracelet, sterling, green glass, and enameling, c. 1925, $225.

Top left: pot metal brooch with green, clear, and topaz rhinestones, c. 1930, $135; bottom left: flower brooch with green glass and rhinestones, c. 1930, $195; top right: butterfly brooch with green and clear rhinestones, c. 1925, $110; bottom right: Art Deco brooch with clear and green rhinestones, c. 1930, $195.

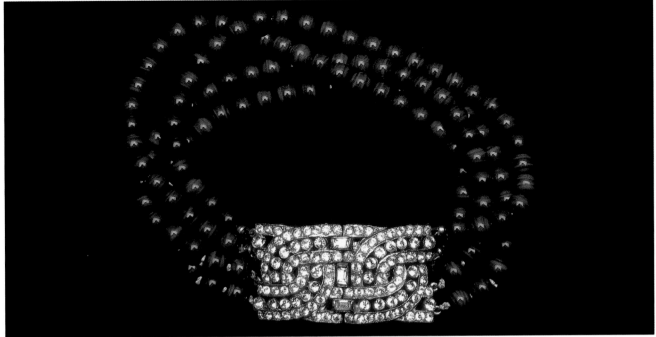

Art Deco bracelet, pot metal, rhinestones, and blue lapis beads, c. 1925, $325.

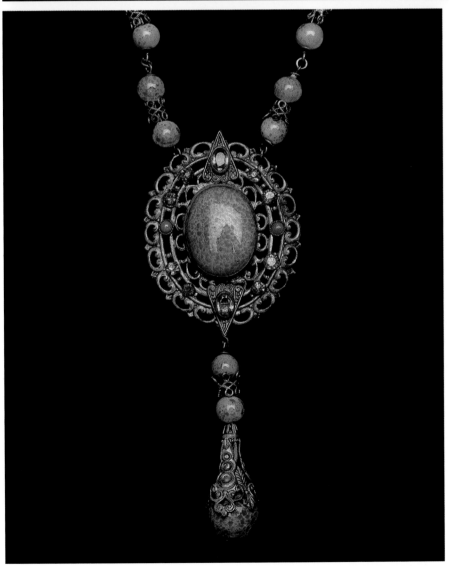

Czechoslovakian necklace, brass, green glass, topaz glass, and pink and topaz rhinestones, c. 1925, $425.

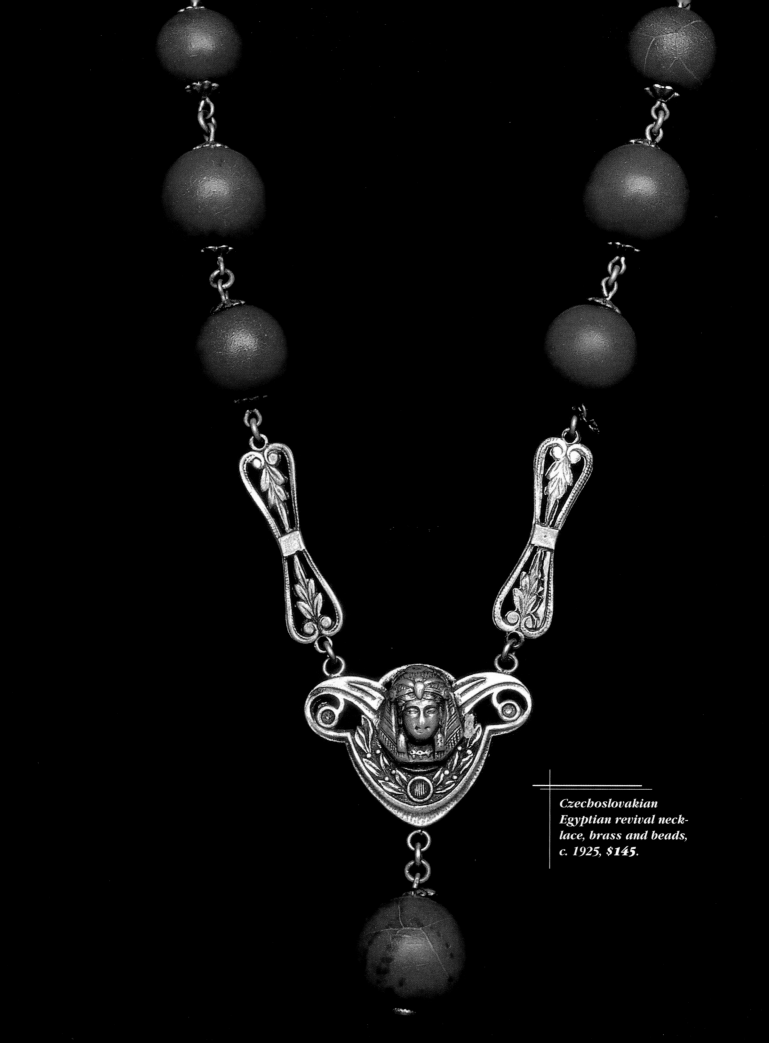

Czechoslovakian Egyptian revival neck-lace, brass and beads, c. 1925, $145.

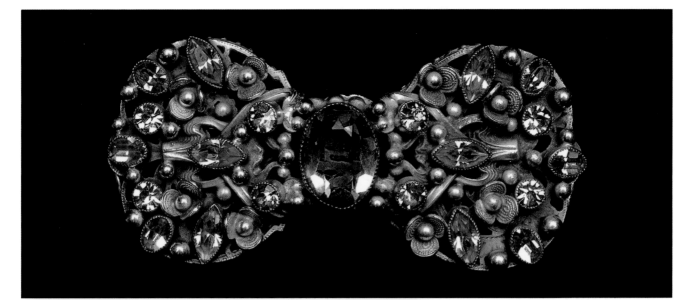

*Czechoslovakian bow brooch, brass and blue glass, c. 1930, **$245**.*

*Czechoslovakian necklace, brass, green glass, topaz glass, and pink and topaz rhinestones, c. 1925, **$425**.*

Czechoslovakian Egyptian revival molded glass necklaces, c. 1925, from left: $225; $185.

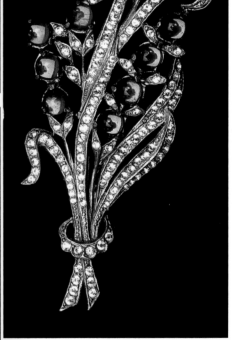

From top: brooch with
rhinestones, c. 1920,
$165; right: floral brooch,
pot metal, rhinestones,
and blue glass
cabochons, c. 1930, *$190*;
bottom left: Art Deco
dress clip, pot metal, and
rhinestones, c. 1930,
$195.

*Czechoslovakian bracelet, brass, green
and amethyst glass, c. 1935, $495.*

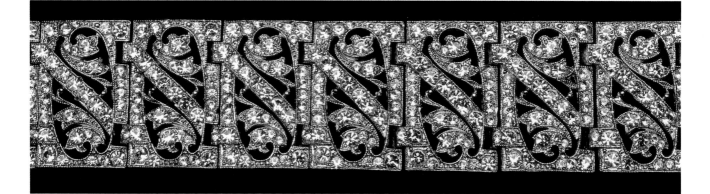

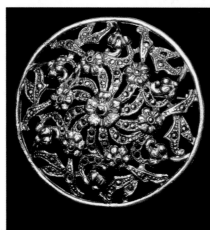

Art Deco bracelet, rhodium, and rhinestones, c. 1920, $425.

Left: sterling brooch with marcasites, c. 1920, $110; right: pot metal brooch with marcasites, blue glass, and enameling, c. 1925, $100.

Art Deco cuff with rhinestones, c. 1920, $225.

Czechoslovakian clover brooch, blue glass and clear rhinestones, c. 1930, $185.

Czechoslovakian pendant and matching bracelet with green glass and enameling, c. 1920s, $395.

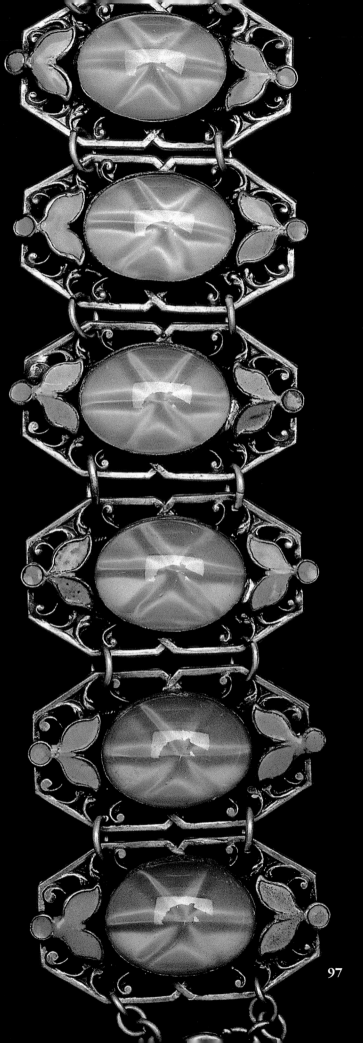

Czechoslovakian Egyptian revival molded glass necklaces, c. 1925, from left: $185; $100.

*Czechoslovakian brooches, c. 1930s, from left: brass with green rhinestone, **$50**; brass with green rhinestones, **$55**; brass with blue rhinestones, **$60**.*

*Left: flower brooch with tremblers, enamel, blue and clear rhinestones, c. 1935, **$145**; middle: flower brooch with trembler, enameling and clear rhinestones, c. 1935, **$115**; right: flower brooch, enameling, clear rhinestones and pink glass beads, c. 1935, **$125**.*

Czechoslovakian Egyptian revival molded glass necklaces, c. 1925, from left: $100; $185; $125.

*Left: bird brooch with clear rhinestones and enameling, c. 1935, **$185**; middle: bird fur clip with clear, pink, and light blue rhinestones, faux pearl, and enameling, **$110**; right: enameled lobster brooch with moveable claws, c. 1935, **$125**.*

*Double flower brooch with trembler, enameling, blue and clear rhinestones, c. 1930, **$195**.*

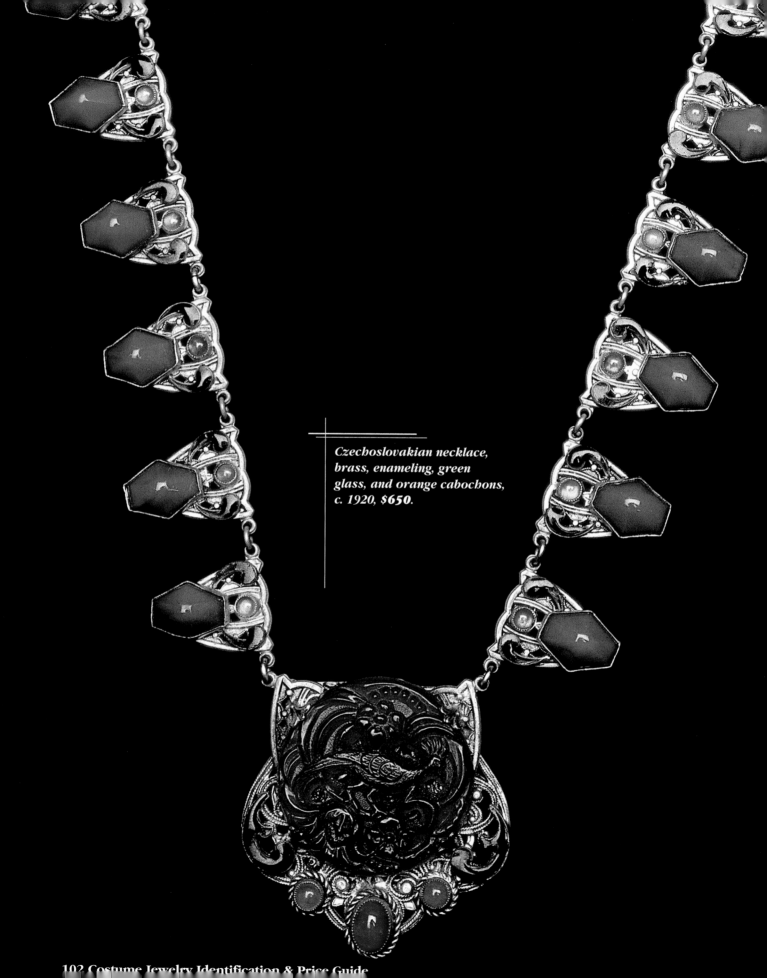

Czechoslovakian necklace, brass, enameling, green glass, and orange cabochons, c. 1920, $650.

Czechoslovakian earrings, brass with enameling and purple glass, c. 1925, $145..

Sailor brooch, enameling, faux pearls and rhinestones, c. 1930, $145.

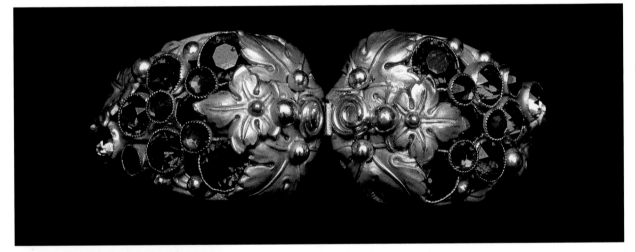

Czechoslovakian hinged bangle, green rhinestones, c. 1930, $125.

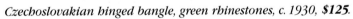

Flower brooch, Rhodium, enameling, clear rhinestones, and blue glass cabochons, c. 1935, $225.

Czechoslovakian necklace, brass, enameling, and glass, c. 1925, $195.

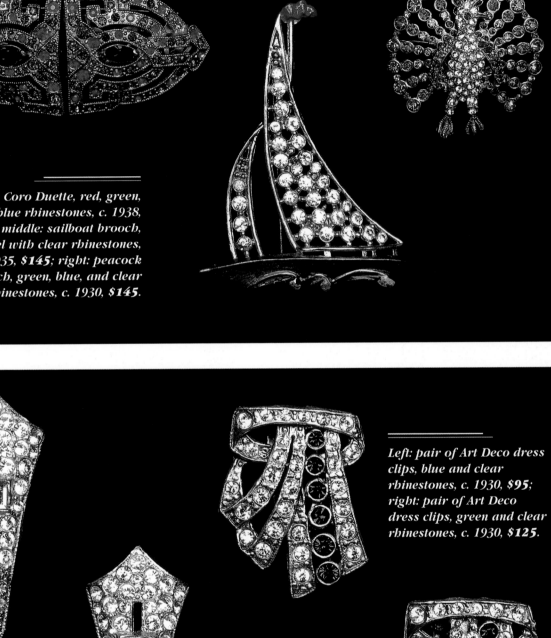

*Left: Coro Duette, red, green, and blue rhinestones, c. 1938, **$125**; middle: sailboat brooch, enamel with clear rhinestones, c. 1935, **$145**; right: peacock brooch, green, blue, and clear rhinestones, c. 1930, **$145**.*

*Left: pair of Art Deco dress clips, blue and clear rhinestones, c. 1930, **$95**; right: pair of Art Deco dress clips, green and clear rhinestones, c. 1930, **$125**.*

Left: flower fur clip, enameling with clear rhinestones and pink cabochons, c. 1935, $145; middle: flower brooch, enameling with clear rhinestones and pink cabochons, c. 1935, $165; right: flower basket brooch, enameling with clear rhinestones and pink cabochons, c. 1930, $145.

Left: flower brooch, enameling with clear, blue, green, red, topaz, and lavender rhinestones, c. 1935, $175; middle: flower dress clip, enameling with clear rhinestones, c. 1930, $50; right: flower brooch, enameling with clear rhinestones, c. 1935, $195.

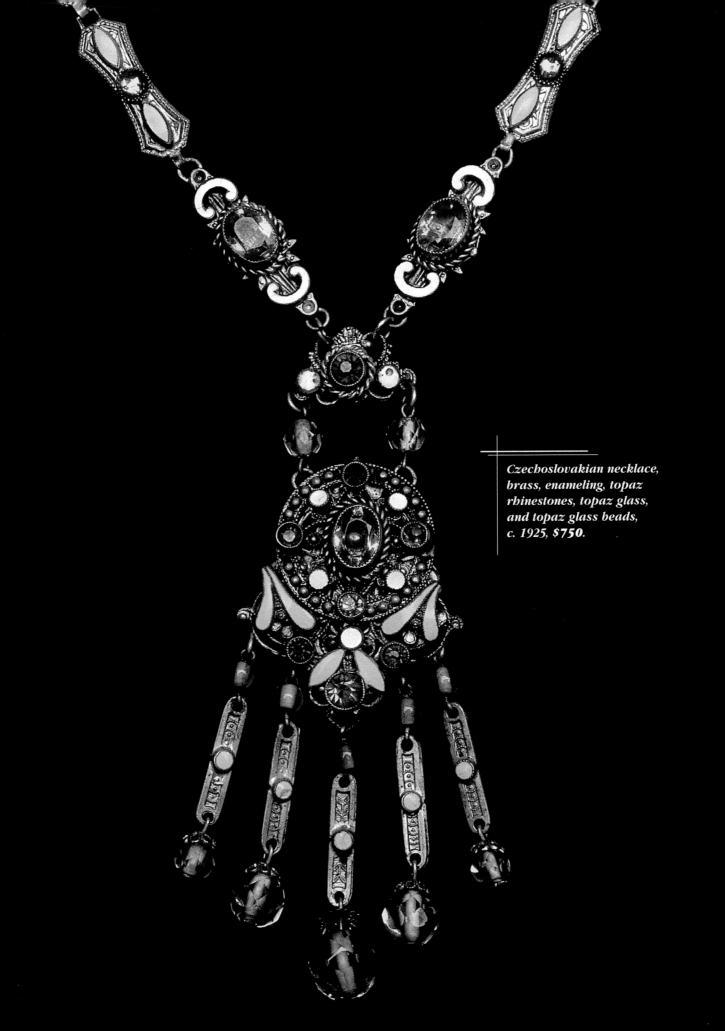

Czechoslovakian necklace, brass, enameling, topaz rhinestones, topaz glass, and topaz glass beads, c. 1925, $750.

Czechoslovakian necklace, silver with blue and clear rhinestones and blue glass cabachon, c. 1930, $165.

Czechoslovakian Egyptian revival necklace, beads, and molded glass beads, c. 1925, $225.

*Left: flower brooch, enameling with pink glass and black rhinestone, c. 1930, **$75**; middle: flower brooch, enameling with green rhinestones, c. 1935, **$100**; right: bird brooch, enameling with pink, clear, and green rhinestones, 1930, **$145**.*

*Left: fish pin, enameling with glass cabochons, c. 1930, **$65**; middle: bow brooch with green, topaz, lavender, and blue glass, c,. 1930, **$70**; right: bird brooch, enameling, clear rhinestones, and amethyst glass, c. 1930, **$125**.*

Left: Czechoslovakian Egyptian revival glass bead necklace, c. 1925, $100; right: Egyptian revival scarab bracelet, c. 1925, $425.

*Left: flower brooch, enameling with clear rhinestones, c. 1930, **$185**; right: flower brooch, enameling with clear rhinestones, c. 1935, **$145**.*

*Egyptian revival wraparound snake bracelet with enameling, c. 1925, **$595**.*

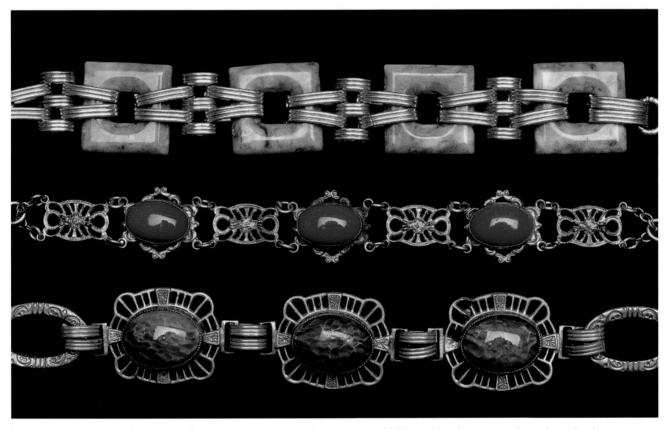

*Top: Czechoslovakian bracelet, yellow metal and green glass, c. 1925, **$225**; middle: Czechoslovakian bracelet, brass, enameling, and red glass, c. 1925, **$125**; bottom: Czechoslovakian bracelet, brass and green glass, c. 1925, **$150**.*

Czechoslovakian necklace, silver with green glass, c. 1930, $225.

Sterling bracelet with rhinestones, blue, green, pink, and topaz glass, Germany, c.1930s, $595.

Art Deco earrings, sterling, rhinestones and red glass, c. 1920, $295.

Art Deco necklace, sterling with enameling, c. 1920, $750.

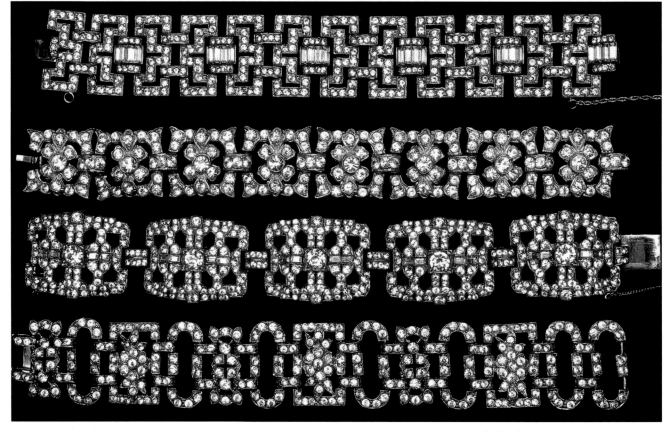

Art Deco bracelets, pot metal, and rhinestones, c. 1920s, from top to bottom: $285; $190; $265; $135.

Art Deco bracelets, pot metal, and rhinestones, c. 1920s, from top to bottom: $395; $185; $465; $425.

Art Deco necklace, marcasites and green glass, c. 1930, $110.

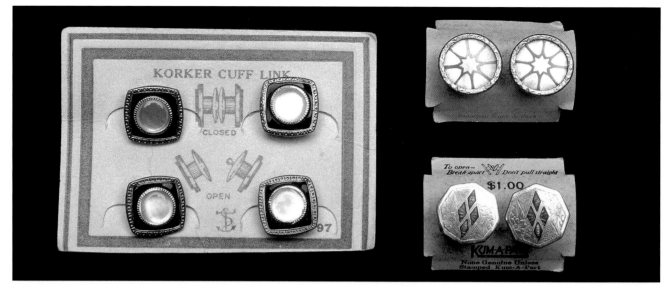

Left: Korker snap cufflinks on original card, c. 1920s, $45; top right: Kum-A-Part snap cufflinks on original card, c.1920s, $45; bottom right: Kum-A-Part snap cufflinks on original card, c. 1920s, $55.

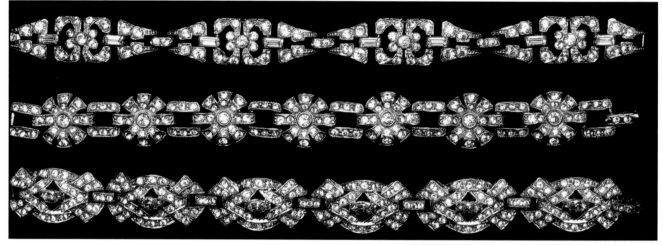

Art Deco bracelets, pot metal, and rhinestones, c. 1920s, from top to bottom: $185; $155; $195.

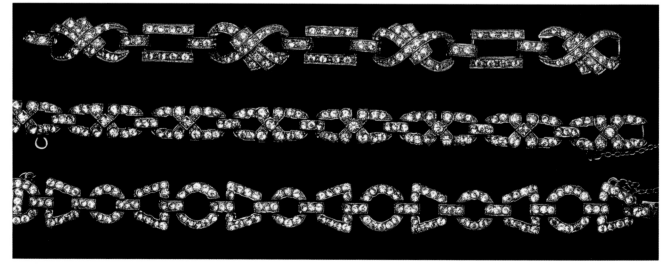

Art Deco bracelets, pot metal, and rhinestones, c. 1920s, from top to bottom: $125; $195; $165.

*Top: Art Deco enamel necklace, c. 1928, **$225**; middle: woman's face brooch, enamel, 1920s, **$85**; bottom: Egyptian revival brooch, enamel, c. 1925, **$450**.*

*Art Deco sautoir, black and clear faceted glass beads and molded glass, c. 1925, **$195**.*

Art Deco necklace, silver metal, enameling, and beads, c. 1925, $195.

*Art Deco earrings, black and coral colored glass beads, c. 1925, **$175**.*

*Art Deco necklace, silver with faux pearls, black beads, black and clear rhinestones and glass, c. 1925, **$245**.*

*Art Deco earrings, blue glass and rhinestones, c. 1925, **$125**.*

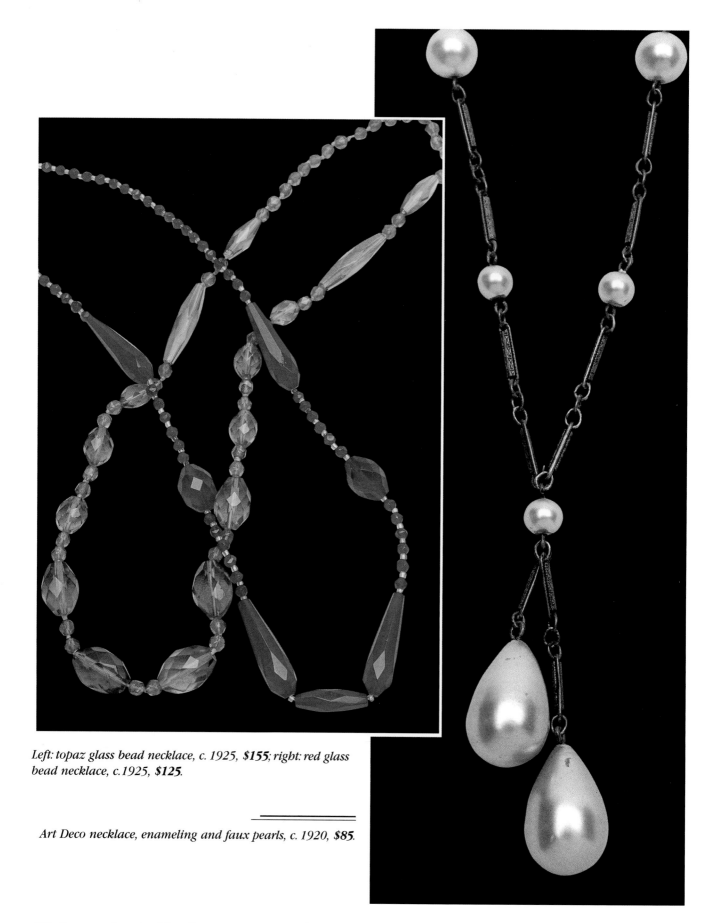

*Left: topaz glass bead necklace, c. 1925, **$155**; right: red glass bead necklace, c.1925, **$125**.*

*Art Deco necklace, enameling and faux pearls, c. 1920, **$85**.*

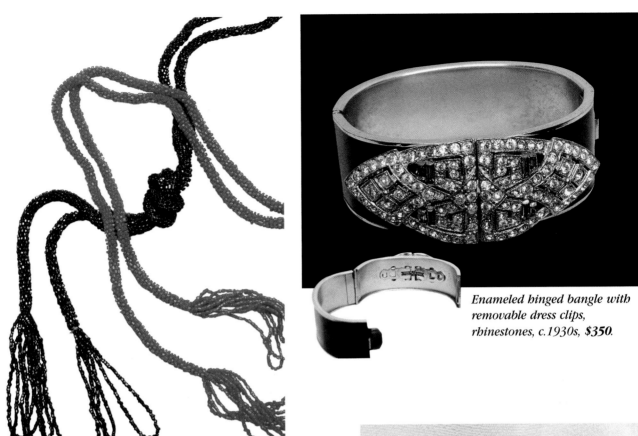

Enameled hinged bangle with removable dress clips, rhinestones, c.1930s, $350.

Negligee necklaces, glass beads, c. 1920s, $110 each.

German Art Deco hinged bangle, mixed metals, Galalith, and rhinestones, c. 1930; $575.

Rhodium hinged bangle with clear rhinestones, pink, blue, and green faceted glass, red cabochons, c. 1935, $595.

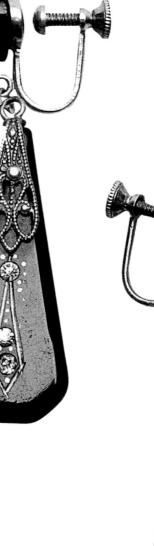

Left: Art Deco Bakelite pendant with rhinestones, c. 1925, **$145**; right: Art Deco Bakelite earrings with rhinestones, c. 1925, **$135**.

Flower brooches with tremblers, c. 1935, from left to right: $125; $170.

Left: flower brooch, goldtone metal with red and clear rhinestones, c. 1935, $155; middle: flower brooch, goldtone metal with green and red glass beads, c. 1935, $165; right: Asian man brooch, enameling with clear rhinestones and beads, c. 1935, $125.

POSTWAR
MODERN

*Sterling pendant
with quartz,
maker's mark
unreadable,
c. 1955, $450.*

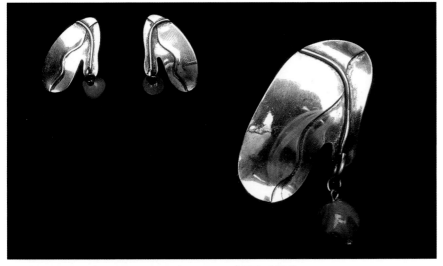

*Sterling pin and earring set with agate, c. 1955, **$225**.*

*Sterling earrings, c. 1960, **$100**.*

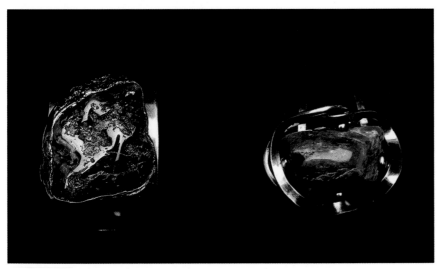

*Left: sterling cuff with stone, c. 1960, **$175**; right: sterling cuff with stone, c. 1960, **$245**.*

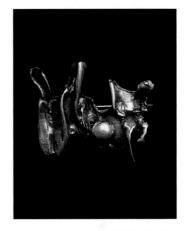

*Sterling brooch, c.1960, **$300**.*

*Left: sterling leaf earrings, Paul Lobel, c.1950s, **$125**; right: sterling leaf brooch, Paul Lobel, c. 1950s, **$250**.*

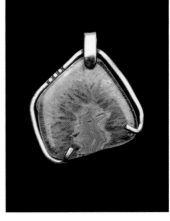

*Sterling pendant with quartz, Henry Steig, c. 1950s, **$250**.*

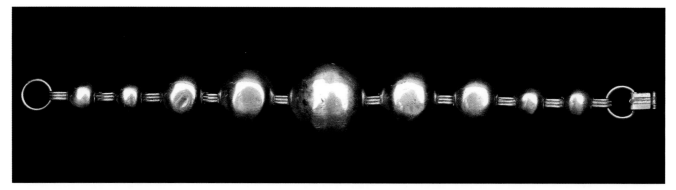

*Sterling bracelet, c. 1955, **$95**.*

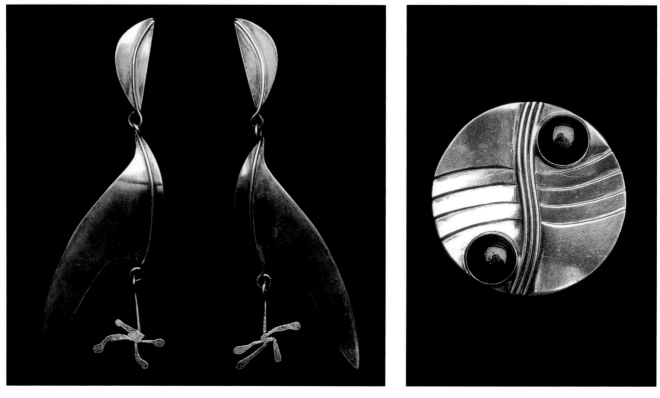

*Sterling earrings, c.1960, **$125**.*

*Sterling brooch with enameling, Esther Lewittes, c. 1950s, **$200**.*

*Sterling Rebajes bracelet, c.1950, **$250**.*

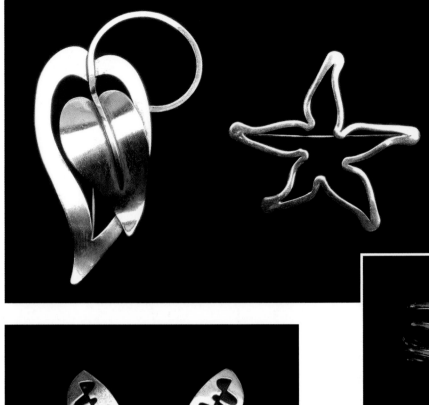

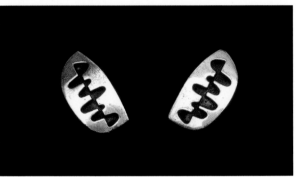

*Left: sterling leaf brooch, Paul Lobel, c.1950, **$250**; right: sterling starfish brooch, Jules Brenner, c. 1950, **$100**.*

*Sterling earrings, Ed Weiner, c. 1950s, **$175**.*

*Sterling cuff bracelet, Henry Steig, c. 1950s, **$300**.*

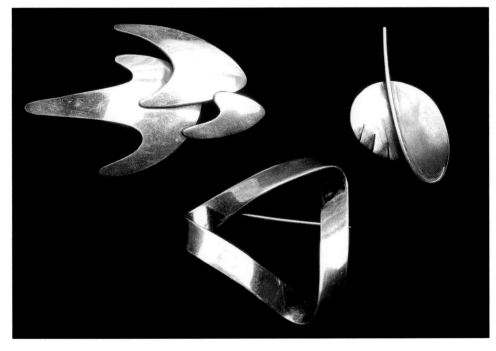

*Top left: sterling boomerang brooch, Henry Steig, c. 1950, **$200**; top right: sterling shadow leaf brooch, Henry Steig, c. 1950, **$100**; bottom: sterling ribbon brooch, Bill Tendler, c. 1950s, **$150**.*

Sterling chain and sterling and wood bird pendant, Ed Levin, c. 1950s, $250.

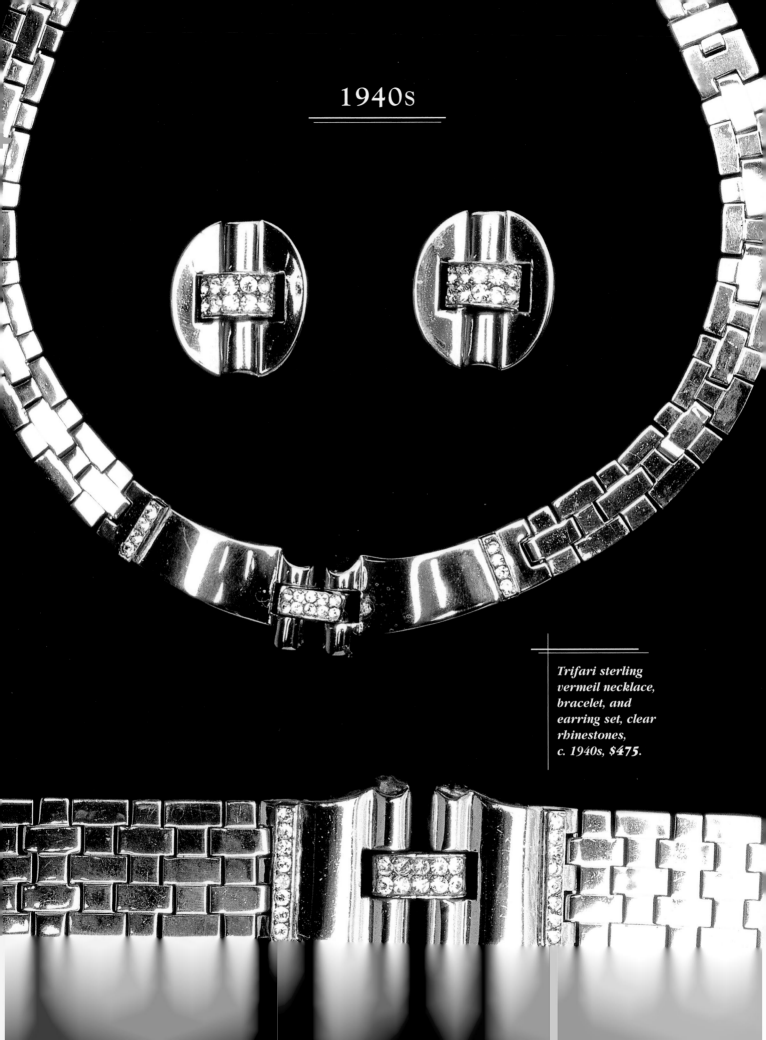

1940s

*Trifari sterling
vermeil necklace,
bracelet, and
earring set, clear
rhinestones,
c. 1940s, $475.*

Sterling floral brooch with pink, topaz and light blue faceted glass, c. 1945, $245.

Sterling vermeil brooch with green glass, c. 1945, $110.

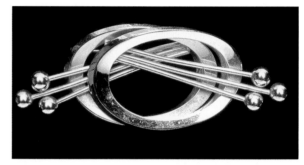

Sterling vermeil brooch, c. 1940, $95.

Sterling vermeil brooch, green glass and rhinestones, c. 1945, $185.

Sterling vermeil flower brooch, clear rhinestones and fuchsia glass. c. 1945, $195.

Sterling vermeil rose brooch, clear rhinestones, c. 1940, $195.

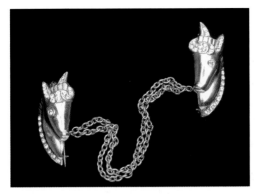

Sterling vermeil horse head brooches connected by chain, pink and clear rhinestones, c. 1945, $125.

Man playing guitar watch pin, Gotham, enameling, c. 1940, $345.

Sterling vermeil bow brooch, clear rhinestones and topaz glass, c. 1940, $245.

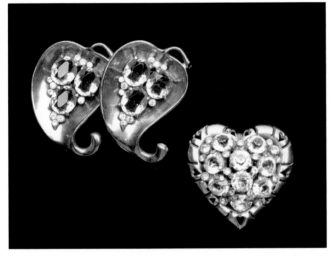

Left: sterling vermeil, double-leaf brooch, clear rhinestones and lavender glass, c. 1945, $195; right: sterling vermeil heart brooch, clear rhinestones, c. 1940, $165.

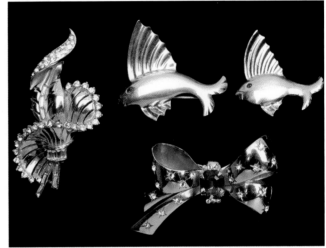

Left: Coro sterling vermeil brooch, clear rhinestones, c. 1940, $125; top right: pair of sterling vermeil fish pins, c. 1948, $75; bottom right: Coro goldtone bow pin, clear and blue rhinestones, c. 1948, $85.

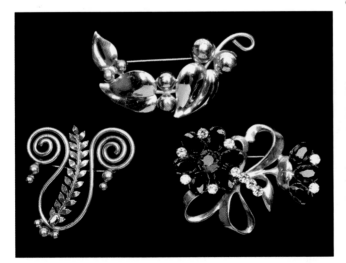

Left: sterling vermeil brooch, red rhinestone, c. 1948, $90; middle: Napier sterling vermeil leaf brooch, c. 1940, $65; right: sterling vermeil flower brooch, green glass and clear rhinestones, c. 1940, $165.

Sterling vermeil bird in cage brooch and earring set, clear, red and green rhinestones, c. 1947, $325.

*Top: sterling vermeil bracelet, c. 1940, **$95**; middle: sterling vermeil bracelet, c. 1942, **$95**; bottom: sterling vermeil bracelet, light blue rhinestone, c. 1946, **$115**.*

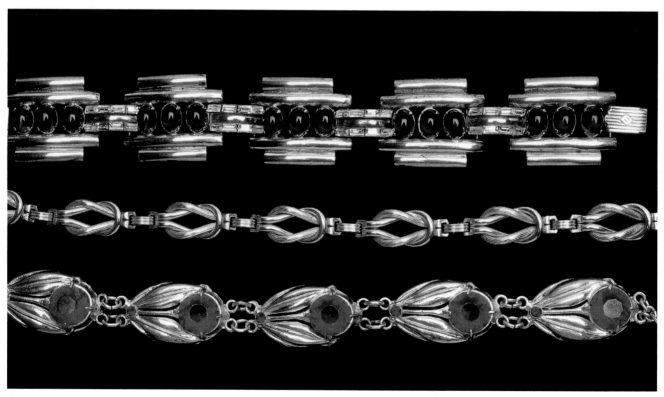

*Top: sterling vermeil bracelet, clear rhinestones and red cabochons, c. 1940, **$195**; middle: twisted rope bracelet, c. 1945, **$95**; bottom: retro bracelet, red rhinestones, c. 1940s, **$145**.*

Sterling vermeil fur clip and earring set, blue glass and clear rhinestones, c. 1945, **$345**.

Sterling vermeil brooch and earring set, clear rhinestones and blue glass, c. 1940, **$165**.

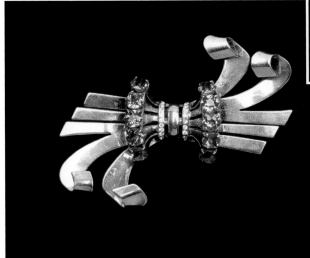

Sterling vermeil bow brooch, clear and pink rhinestones, c. 1945, **$195**.

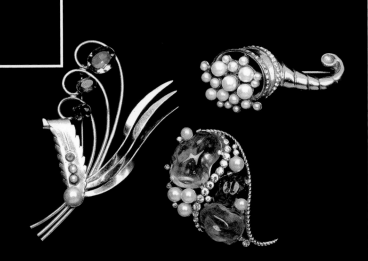

Sterling vermeil brooch, faux pearls and amethyst glass, missing one faux pearl, c. 1942, **$95**; top right: horn of plenty brooch, faux pearls and rhinestones, c. 1948, **$100**; bottom right: sterling vermeil brooch, clear rhinestones, faux pearls, pink, and amethyst glass, c. 1948, **$140**.

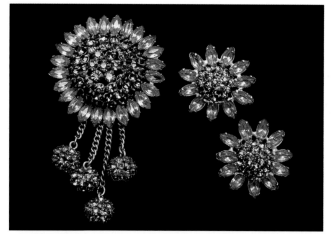

*Sterling vermeil brooch and earring set, blue and amethyst rhinestones, c. 1945, **$225.***

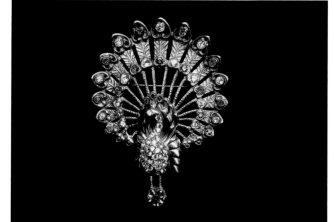

*Sterling vermeil peacock brooch, clear and blue rhinestones, c. 1948, **$245.***

*Sterling vermeil dress clip, blue and clear rhinestones, c. 1940, **$110.***

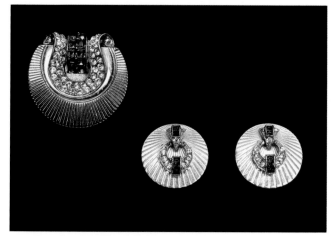

*Boucher fur clip and earring set, clear and blue rhinestones, c. 1945, **$265.***

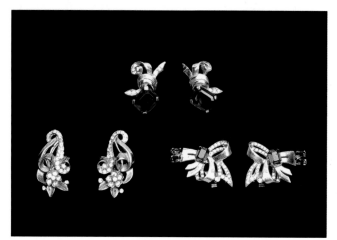

*Top: sterling vermeil earrings, clear rhinestones and amethyst glass, c. 1940, **$125**; bottom left: sterling vermeil floral design earrings, rhinestones, c. 1940, **$110**; bottom right: Mazer sterling vermeil earrings, green glass and clear rhinestones, c. 1940, **$155.***

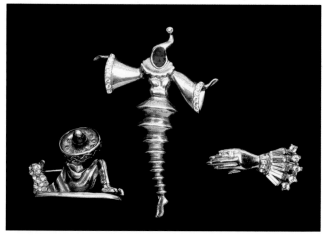

*Left: Mexican design pin, fuchsia and green rhinestones, c. 1940, **$40**; middle: sterling vermeil brooch, clear, and red rhinestones, c. 1940, **$135**; right: sterling vermeil hand brooch, clear rhinestones, c. 1948, **$125.***

*Trifari sterling
vermeil necklace
and bracelet set,
blue glass and
clear rhinestones,
c. 1940, $490.*

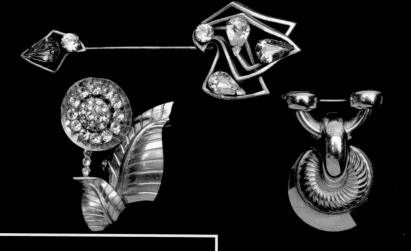

Top: brooch, clear and light blue rhinestones, c. 1948, $95; bottom left: sterling vermeil flower brooch, clear rhinestones, c. 1946, $145; bottom right: Monet sterling vermeil brooch, c. 1940, $80.

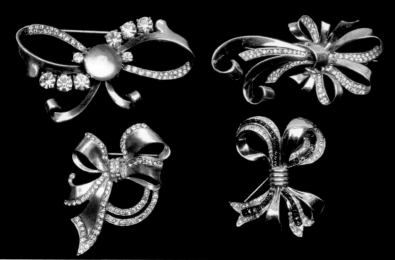

Top left: Mazer sterling vermeil bow brooch, clear rhinestones and blue glass, c. 1945, $165; top right: Mazer sterling vermeil bow brooch, clear rhinestones, c. 1945, $185; bottom left: sterling vermeil bow brooch, c. 1940, $100; bottom right: Boucher sterling vermeil bow brooch, clear and blue rhinestones, c. 1945, $195.

Left: pair of cowboy and cowgirl brooches, sterling vermeil, c. 1940, $135; middle: sterling vermeil Geisha brooch, blue rhinestones, c. 1948, $135; right: sterling vermeil brooch, clear, blue, and light-blue rhinestones, c. 1948, $225.

Elephant brooch, sterling, c. 1940, $195.

Floral hinged bangle, clear rhinestones, c. 1945, $295.

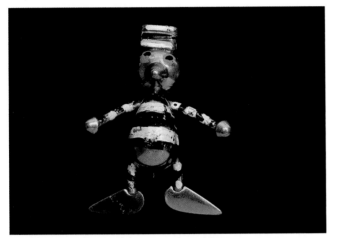

Novelty pin, hand painted, c. 1940, $65.

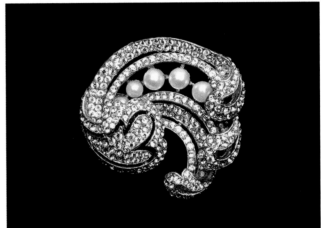

Rhinestone and faux pearl brooch, c. 1949, $165.

Left: Boucher sterling vermeil ballerina brooch, clear rhinestones, c. 1940, $150; right: sterling vermeil dancer brooch, clear rhinestones, green, and red cabochons, c. 1945, $135.

Sterling vermeil brooch and earring set, clear rhinestones, c. 1940, $215.

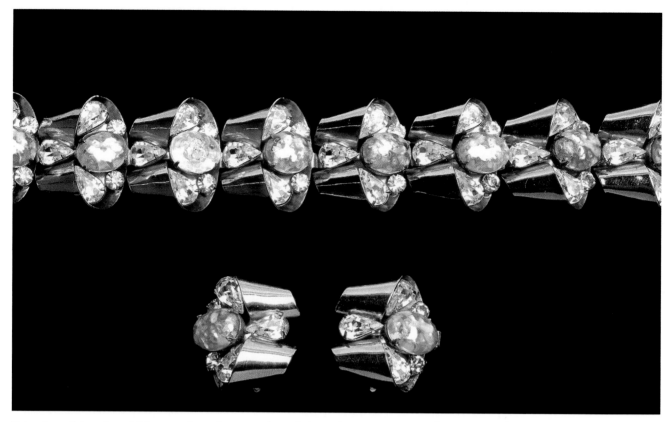

*Retro bracelet and matching earrings, faux pearls and clear rhinestones, c. 1946, **$225**.*

*Top: Mazer sterling vermeil bracelet, clear rhinestones, c. 1940, **$145**; middle: Mazer Bros. bracelet, clear rhinestones, c. 1940, **$160**; bottom: Mazer sterling vermeil bracelet, clear and blue rhinestones, c. 1940, **$160**.*

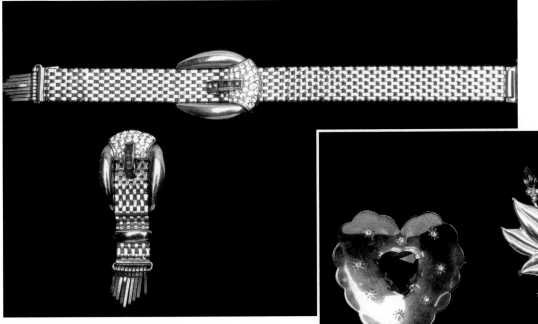

Sterling vermeil buckle bracelet and matching fur clip, red and clear rhinestones, c. 1940, **$460**.

Left: sterling vermeil heart brooch, clear and blue rhinestones, c. 1944, **$125**; right: floral brooch, blue rhinestones, c. 1948, **$90**.

Top left: sterling vermeil flower brooch, topaz glass and clear rhinestones, c. 1940, **$185**; top right: Boucher sterling vermeil brooch, clear rhinestones and amethyst glass, c. 1940, **$225**; bottom left: sterling vermeil brooch, clear rhinestones and amethyst glass, c. 1945, **$100**; bottom right: brooch, clear rhinestones and green glass, c. 1948, **$184**.

Top left: Trifari duck brooch, clear rhinestones and red cabachon, c. 1940s, **$80**; top right: sterling vermeil fish brooch, clear rhinestones, c. 1942, **$225**; bottom left: sterling vermeil bird brooch, blue and clear rhinestones, c. 1944, **$140**; bottom middle: sterling vermeil horse brooch, clear rhinestones, c. 1940s, **$100**; bottom right: sterling vermeil fish brooch, topaz glass and clear rhinestones, c. 1944, **$185**.

1950s

Necklace with clear, light blue, peridot, lavender, and light yellow rhinestones, c.1955, $85.

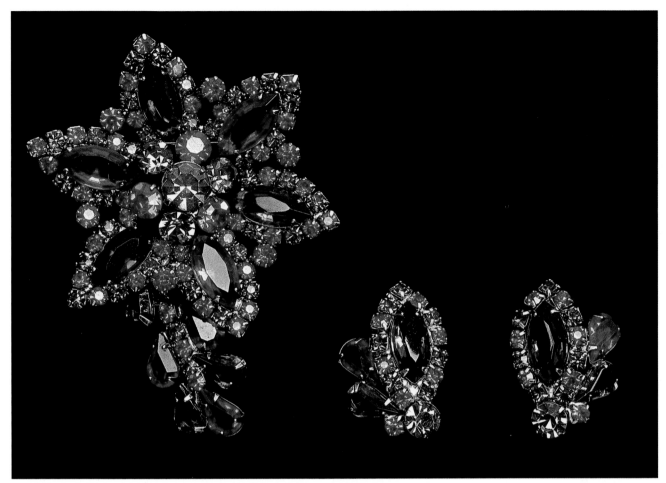

*Brooch and earring set, fuchsia and purple rhinestones, c. 1950s, **$185**.*

*Bracelet, faux pearls, pink and blue rhinestones, missing one rhinestone, c. 1950s, **$145**.*

*Flower brooch, green and clear rhinestones, c. 1950s, **$85**.*

*Rhinestone earrings, c. 1950s, **$70**.*

*Lavender and dark-purple rhinestone brooch, c. 1950s, **$145**.*

*Copper and enamel bracelet with leaf accents, c. 1950s, **$145**.*

Faceted blue glass bead necklace, earring, and bracelet set, c.1959, **$65**.

Necklace with smoke and clear rhinestones, c. 1950s, **$185**.

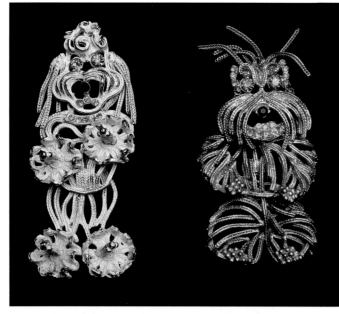

Fringe dog pendants with topaz and black rhinestones, c. 1950s, $95 each.

Earrings with pink and blue glass, clear rhinestones and floral design glass cabochons, c.1958, $95.

Renoir copper cuff and earring set, c. 1950s, $95.

Brooch and earring set, topaz, citrine, and peridot rhinestones, c. 1950s, $95.

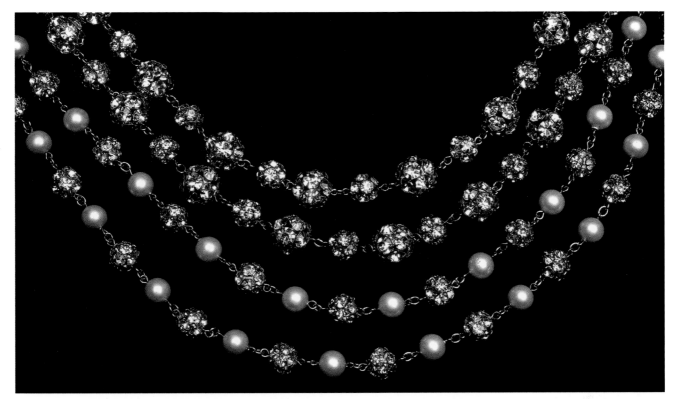

Four-strand necklace with clear rhinestone rhondelles and faux pearls, c. 1950s, $395.

Necklace with faux pearls, crystal beads, and aurora borealis rhinestones, c. 1958, $85.

Aurora borealis necklace and earring set, c. 1955, $60.

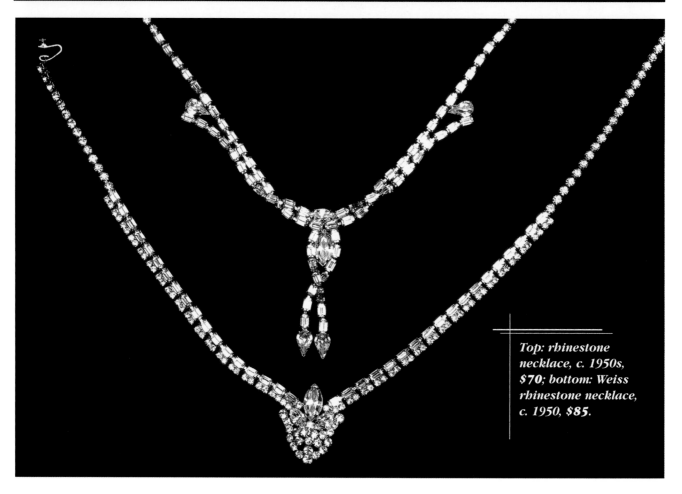

Top: rhinestone necklace, c. 1950s, $70; bottom: Weiss rhinestone necklace, c. 1950, $85.

*Rhinestone earrings, c. 1950s, left: **$30**; right: **$65**.*

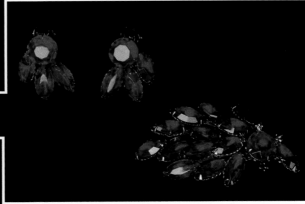

*Brooch and earring set, c. 1950s, **$40**.*

*Left: earrings with blue and aurora borealis rhinestones, c. 1955, **$55**; right: earrings with green and clear rhinestones, c. 1952, **$65**.*

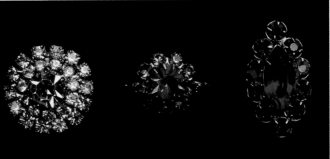

*Rings, c. 1950s, left: clear and light-blue rhinestones, **$25**; middle: blue rhinestones, **$10**; right: red rhinestones, **$20**.*

*Brooch and earring set, blue, light blue and aurora borealis rhinestones, c. 1950s, **$125**.*

*Left: red rhinestone brooch, c. 1950s, **$30**; middle: earrings with red and pink rhinestones, c.1950s, **$30**; right: red rhinestone earrings, c.1950s, **$20**.*

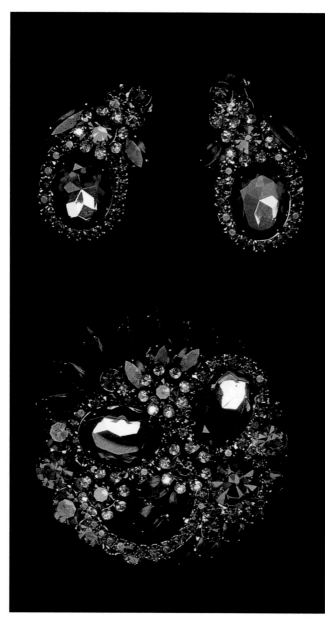

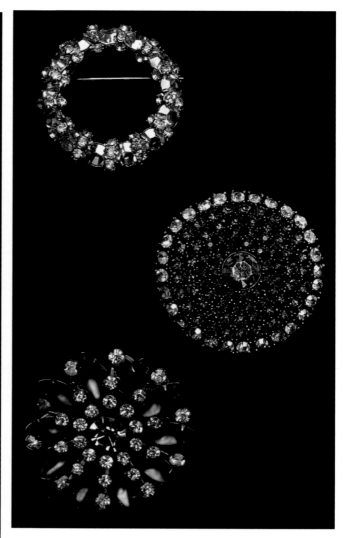

Top: Warner brooch, aurora borealis rhinestones, c.1958, $70; middle: brooch with aurora borealis and purple rhinestones, c. 1955, $30; bottom: flower brooch with grey and clear rhinestones, c.1950s, $30.

Brooch and earring set, blue, green, and aurora borealis rhinestones, c.1950s, $225.

Prom-style rhinestone necklace, c. 1950s, $30.

Brooch and bracelet set, light blue and aurora borealis rhinestones, c. 1955, $125.

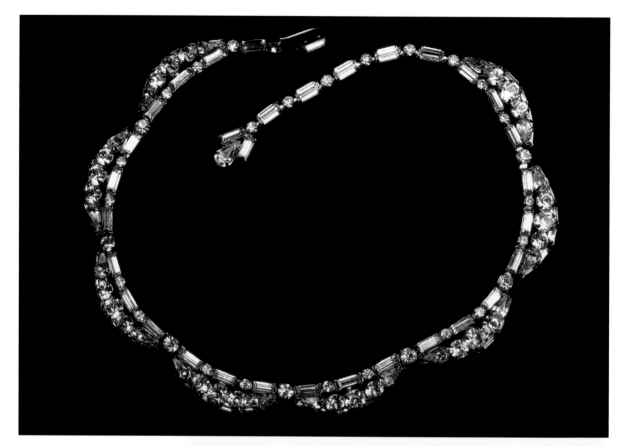

Clear rhinestone necklace,
c. 1955, $95.

Necklace with white
and clear rhinestones,
c. 1950s, $42.

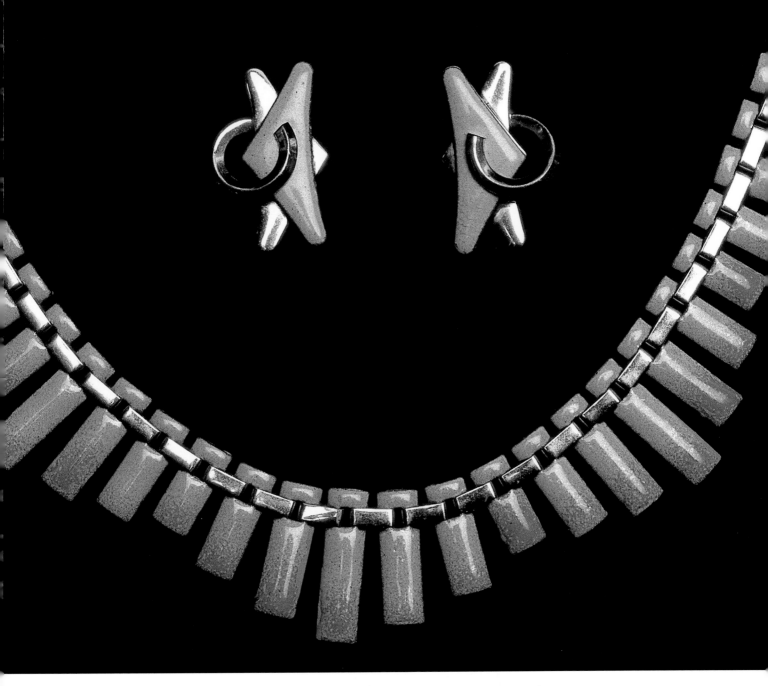

*Top: Matisse enameled earrings, c. 1955, **$40**; bottom: Matisse enameled necklace, c. 1955, **$85**.*

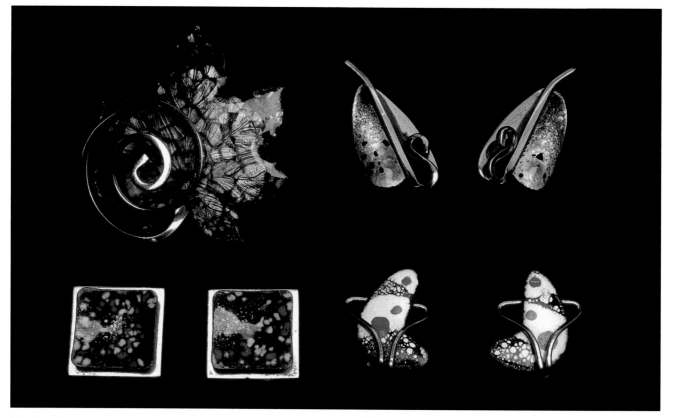

Top left: Renoir Matisse enameled leaf brooch, c. 1955, $65; top right: Renoir Matisse enameled-leaf earrings, c. 1955, $40; bottom left: Matisse enameled earrings, c. 1955, $30; bottom right: Matisse enameled earrings, c.1955, $30.

Necklace with light blue rhinestones, c. 1950s, $115.

Top: rhinestone bracelet, c. 1950, $30; Middle: Prom style rhinestone necklace, c. 1950s, $30; bottom: prom-style rhinestone necklace, c. 1950s, $20.

Lariat-style necklace, clear rhinestones, c. 1950s, $395.

1960s & 1970s

Lion's head doorknocker pendant on goldtone chain, c. 1960s/1970s, $145.

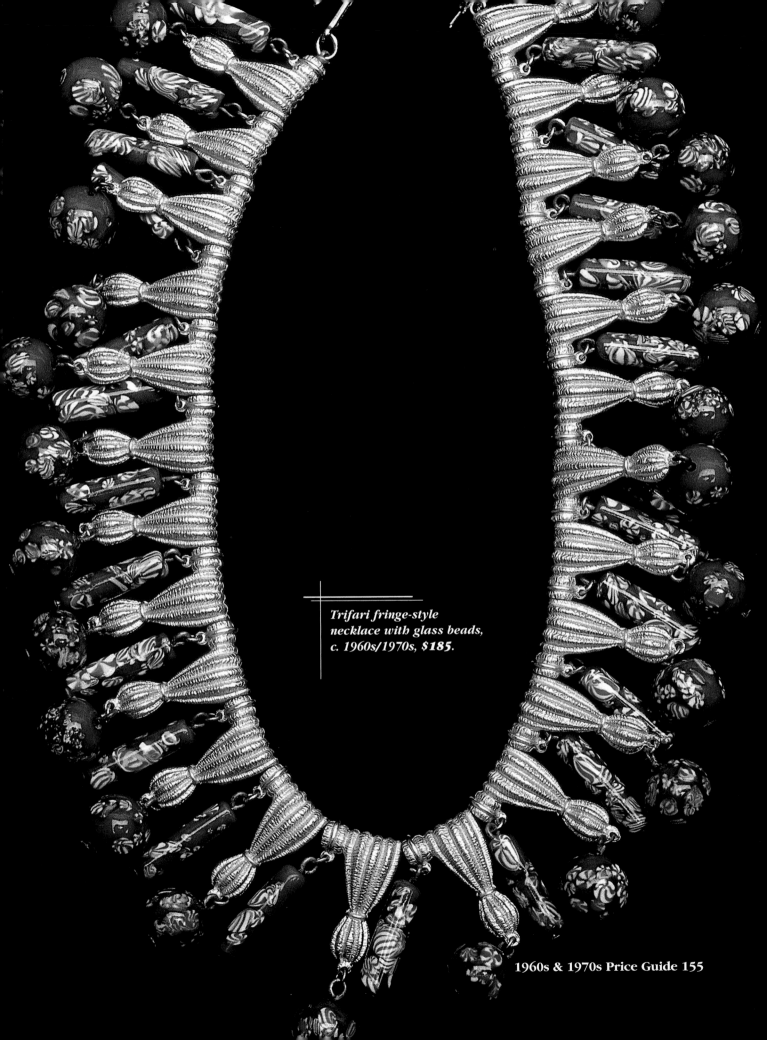

*Trifari fringe-style
necklace with glass beads,
c. 1960s/1970s, $185.*

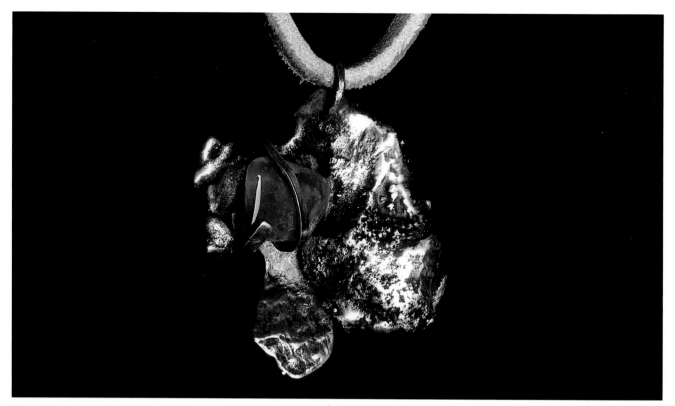

*Sterling and quartz pendant on leather cord, c.1968, **$165**.*

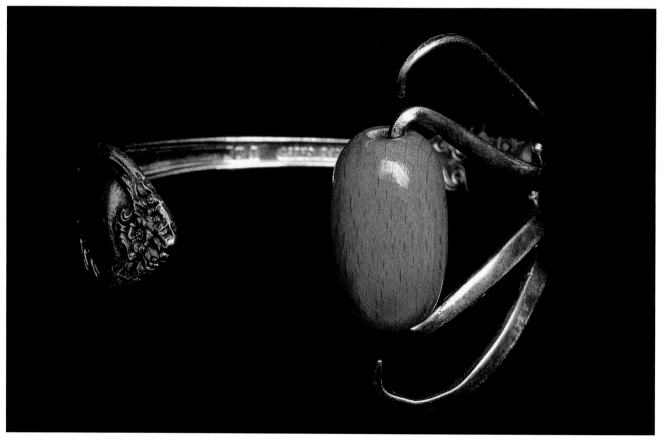

*Handmade spoon cuff with wood bead, c.1966, **$85**.*

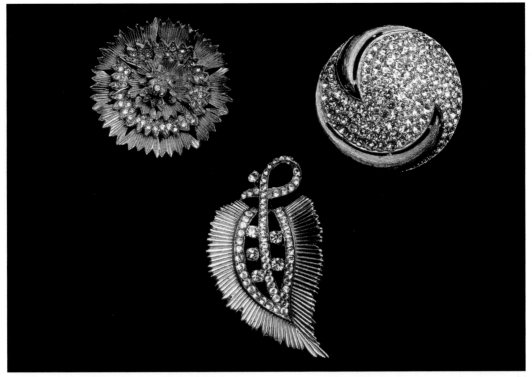

Left: Nettie Rosenstein brooch with rhinestones, c. 1960s, $85; middle: Jomaz leaf brooch with rhinestones, c. 1960s, $125; right: JJ rhinestone brooch, c. 1960s, $30.

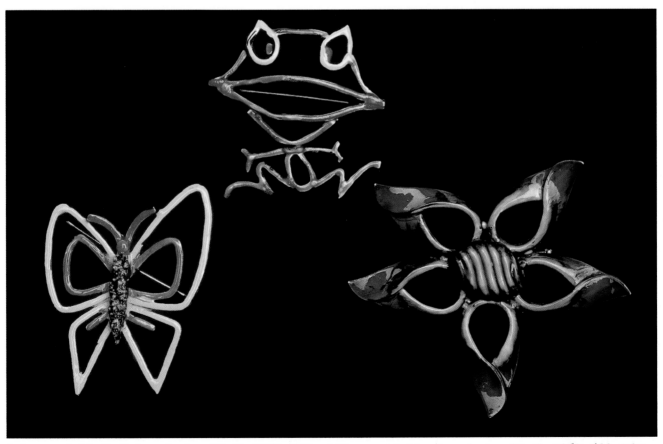

Left: enameled butterfly brooch, signed "Art," c. 1960s, $30; middle: enameled frog brooch, signed "Art," c. 1960s, $30; right: enameled flower brooch, signed "Original by Robert," c. 1960s, $35.

Necklace with green glass and faux pearls, c. 1968, $125.

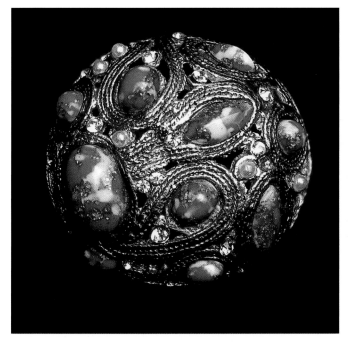

*Brooch with faux turquoise, faux pearls, and rhinestones, c. 1965, **$50**.*

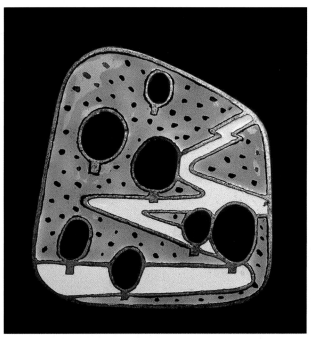

*Modern design enameled brooch, c. 1965, **$165**.*

*Leaf brooch with dangling faux pearls, c. 1965, **$60**.*

*Trifari leaf-design brooch and earring set, c. 1960s, **$40**.*

*Left: sterling hinged bangle, c. 1965, **$95**; right: sterling cuff with brass coil, c. 1965, **$65**.*

*Sterling ring, c. 1968, **$165**.*

Coil design sterling necklace, c. 1960, **$95**.

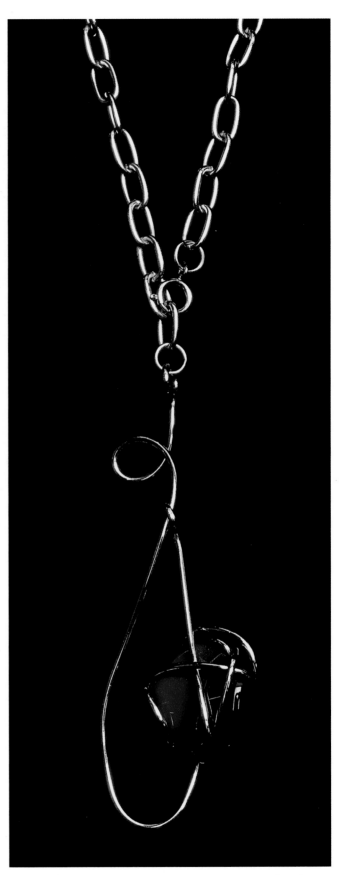

Hand-wrought necklace with polished stone, c. 1960s, **$185**.

Etruscan revival necklace with topaz glass, c. 1968, $110.

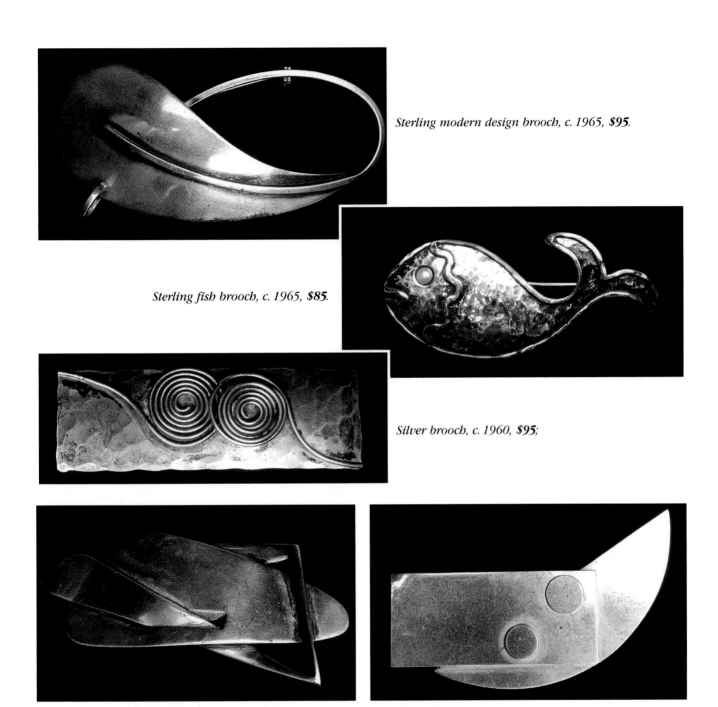

*Sterling modern design brooch, c. 1965, **$95**.*

*Sterling fish brooch, c. 1965, **$85**.*

*Silver brooch, c. 1960, **$95**;*

*Sterling modern design brooch, c. 1960, **$95**.*

*Sterling brooch, c. 1965, **$95**.*

*Sterling rings, 1960s, from left: **$55**; **$65**; **$85**.*

Fringe-style necklace and matching earring set with glass disks, goldtone leaves, blue, burgundy, and yellow beads, c. 1960s/1970s, $50.

*Handmade Denmark pendant on chain with green glass,
c. 1960s, **$195**.*

*Silvertone pendant on chain with faux turquoise,
c. 1966, **$30**.*

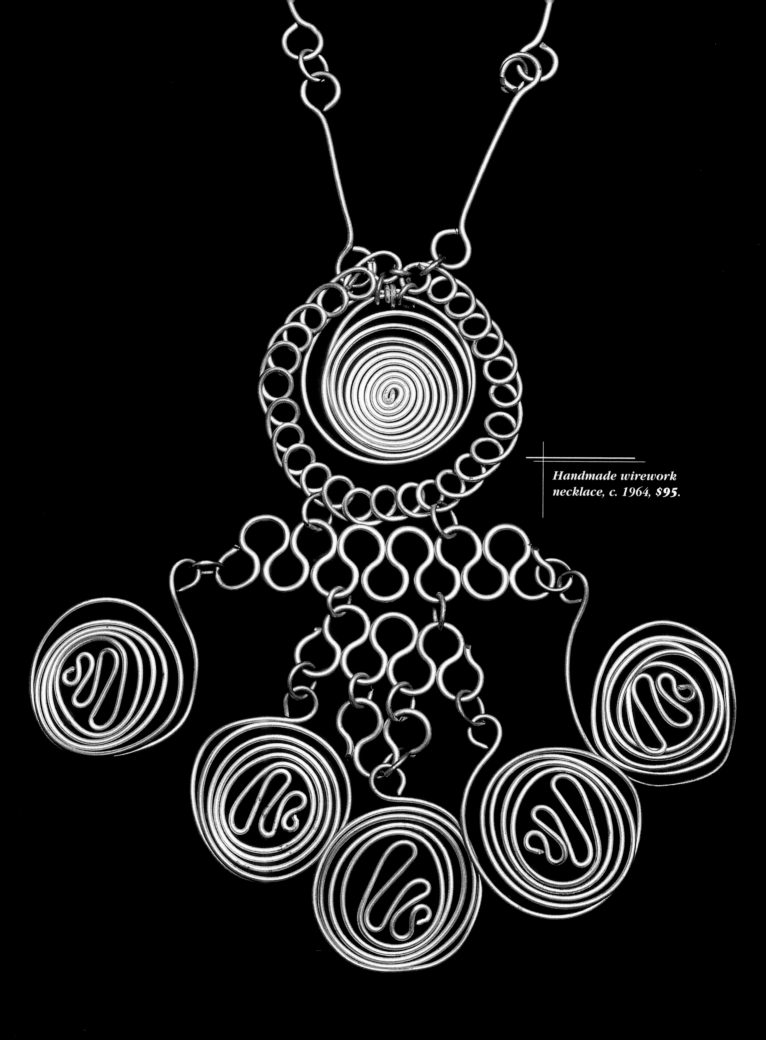

Handmade wirework necklace, c. 1964, $95.

Ankh pendant perfume holder on chain, ceramic, c. 1965, $45.

Flower design pendant on chain with black and clear rhinestones, c.1960s/1970s, $65.

Multi-chain necklace with red, yellow, and blue glass beads, c. 1969, $35.

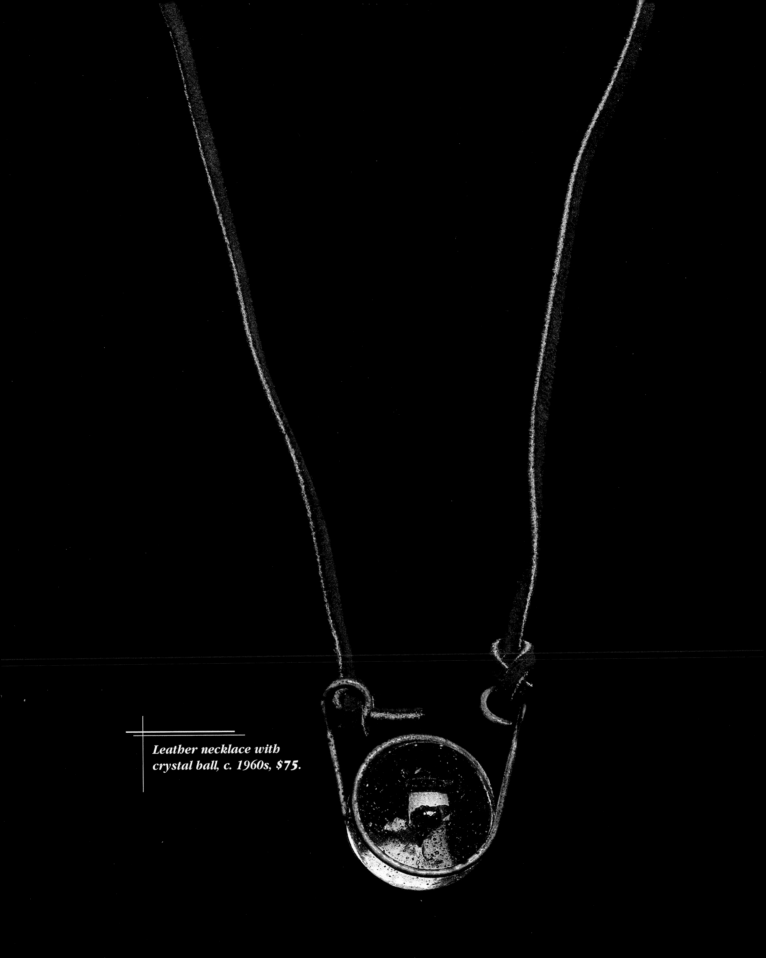

Leather necklace with
crystal ball, c. 1960s, $75.

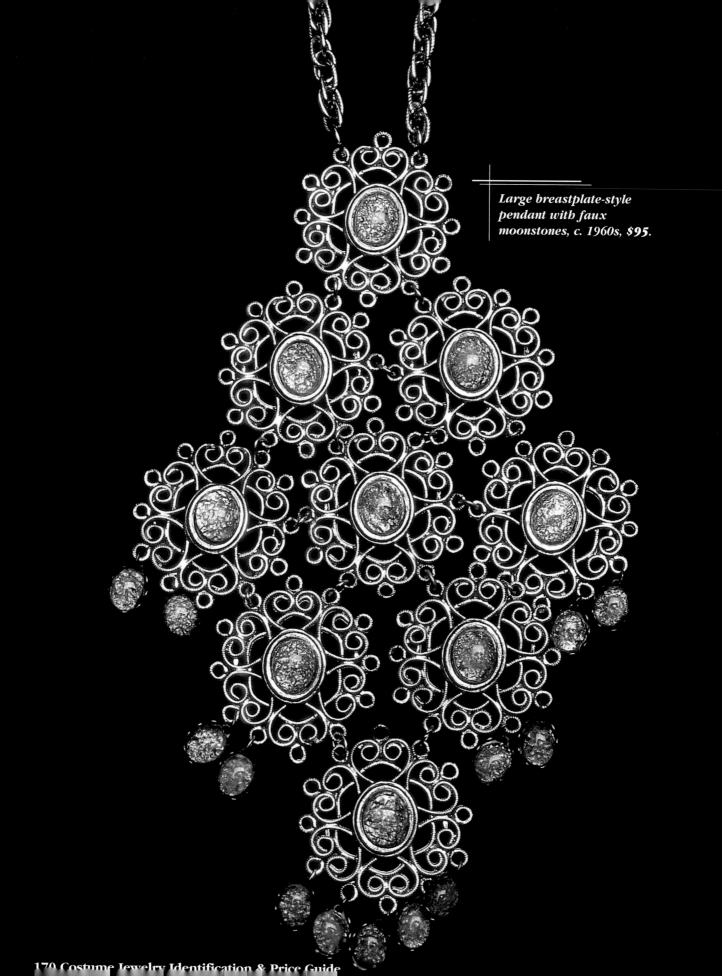

Large breastplate-style pendant with faux moonstones, c. 1960s, $95.

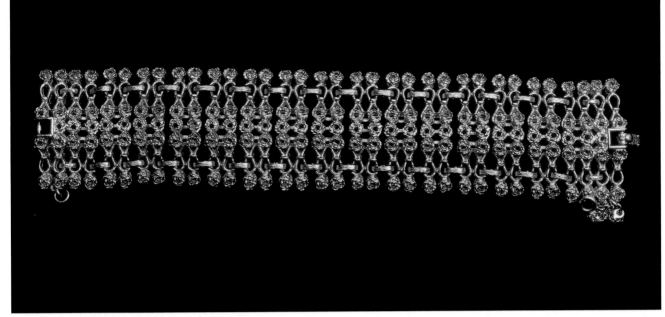

*Goldtone bracelet, signed Monet, c. 1960s, **$40**.*

*Top left: bug brooch with trembling wings, clear rhinestones and faux turquoise, c. 1966, **$45**; top right: leaf brooch with clear rhinestones, c. 1968, **$55**; bottom left: elephant brooch with faux turquoise, green and black rhinestones, c. 1965, **$50**; bottom right: owl brooch with red and clear rhinestones, c. 1968, **$40**.*

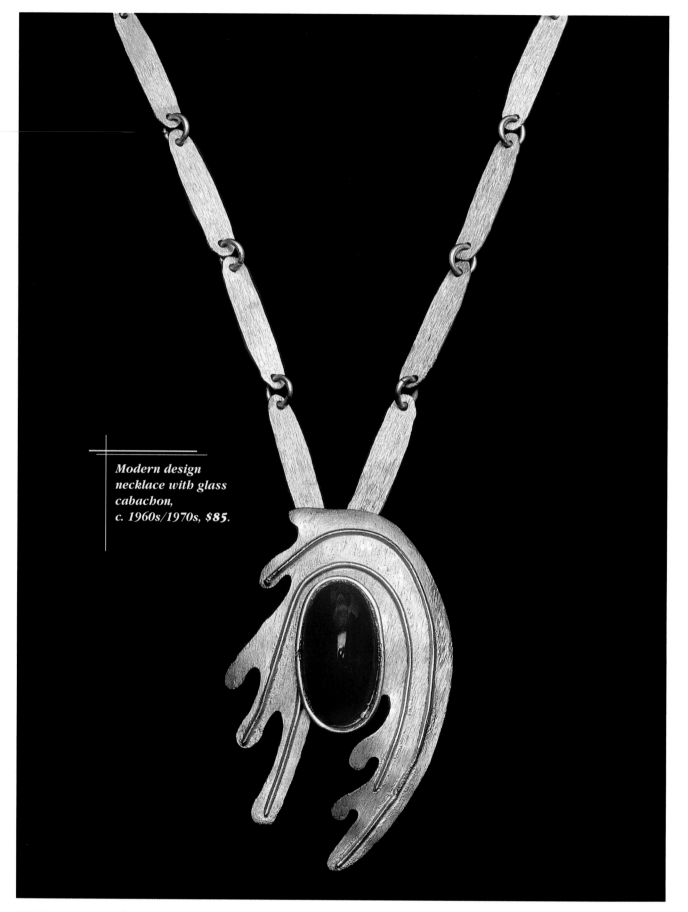

*Modern design
necklace with glass
cabochon,
c. 1960s/1970s, $85.*

Miriam Haskell necklace with faux pearls, blue beads, blue glass, and light-blue rhinestone, c. 1950s, $495.

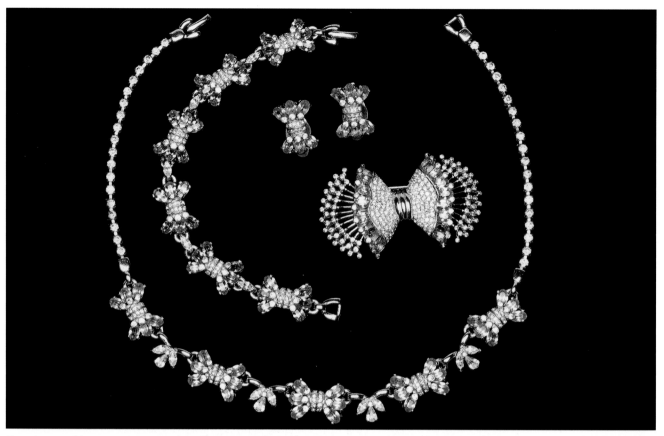

Pennino necklace, earrings, bracelet, and brooch set with clear rhinestones and blue open-back rhinestones, c.1940s, $875.

Regency brooches, c. late1950s, from left: butterfly with topaz, orange, citrine and aurora borealis rhinestones, $135; opaque cabochons and citrine and topaz rhinestones, $160; flower with citrine and aurora borealis rhinestones, $125.

Corocraft sterling jelly belly fish brooch with clear and pink rhinestones and enameling, c. 1940s, *$495*.

Eisenberg eagle brooch with clear rhinestones and enameling, c.1930s, $650.

Coro owl Duette with enameling and rhinestones, c.1940s, $345.

Coro sterling brooch, dog and bird design, c.1955, $165.

Trifari fur clip with green, white and red enameling, clear rhinestones and light-blue, open-back rhinestones, c. 1930s, $495.

Hobe necklace, bracelet and earring set with green, clear, citrine, and aurora borealis rhinestones, c. 1950s, $295.

Alfred Philippe necklace with clear and red rhinestones, c. 1930s, **$625***.*

Trifari necklace with citrine, clear and blue rhinestones, c.1950s, **$195***.*

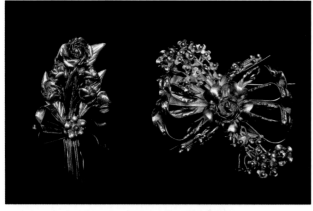

*Hobe sterling brooches, from left: **$195**; **$295**.*

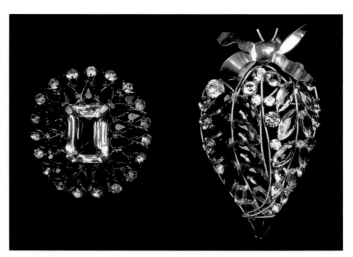

*Left: Vogue sterling brooch with clear and blue rhinestones and glass, c. 1940s, **$195**; right: Vogue sterling vermeil brooch with watermelon rhinestones and amethyst and clear glass, **$225**.*

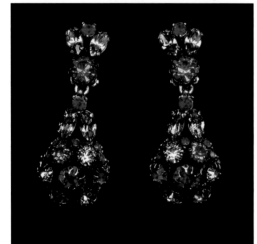

*Schiaparelli earrings with red, orange, and citrine rhinestones, c. 1950s, **$225**.*

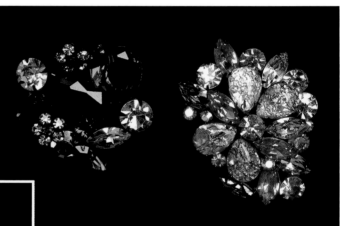

*Regency brooches, c. 1950s, from left: green rhinestones, **$125**; pink and lavender rhinestones, **$115**.*

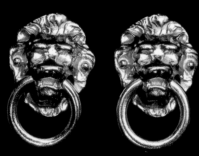

*Kenneth Lane lion door knocker earrings, c. 1960s, **$125**.*

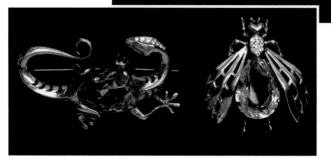

*Left: Reja sterling lizard brooch with blue glass and red rhinestone, c. 1940s, **$265**; Right: Reja sterling bug brooch with blue glass and red and clear rhinestones, c. 1940s, **$185**.*

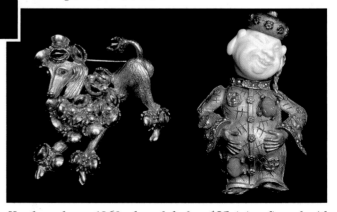

*Har brooches, c. 1960s, from left: dog, **$85**; Asian figural with green glass and red aurora borealis rhinestones, **$265**.*

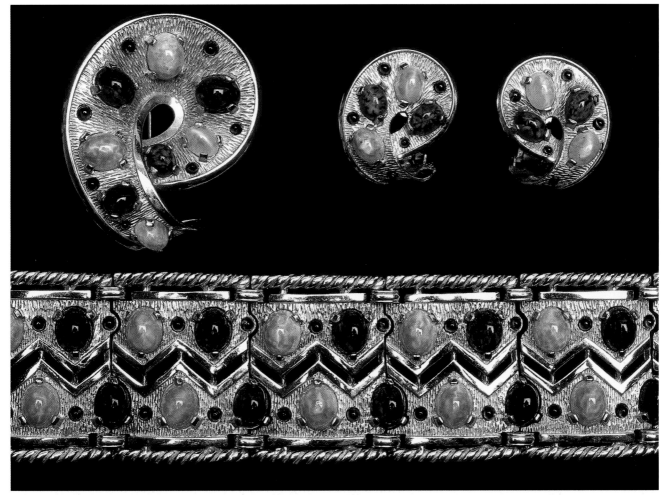

Boucher bracelet, earring and brooch set with purple, blue and pink glass cabochons, c. 1960s, $495.

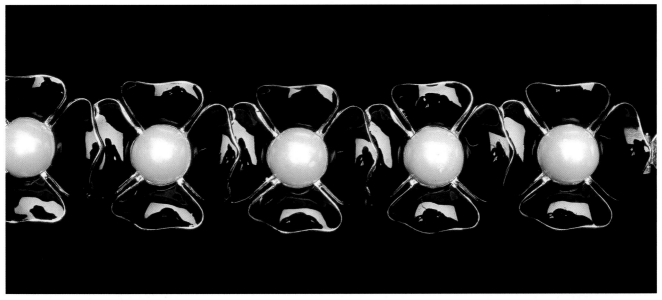

Valentino enameled flower bracelet with faux pearls, c.1960s, $325.

Left: Miriam Haskell cross with faux pearls, c. 1950s, $225; right: Chanel pendant on chain with pink and blue glass and faux pearls, c.1950s, $450.

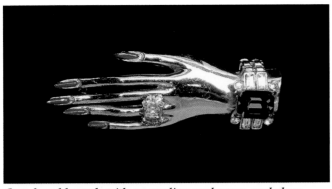

*Coro hand brooch with enameling and green and clear rhinestones, c. 1930s, **$145**.*

*Corocraft sterling enameled flower brooch with clear rhinestones, c. 1940s, **$325**.*

*Left: Eisenberg Original, sterling with rhinestones, c.1930s, **$175**; right: Eisenberg Original, faux pearls, blue and clear rhinestones, c.1930s, missing one baguette, **$395**.*

*Left: Reja brooch with blue glass and clear rhinestones, c. 1930s, **$210**; right: Staret rhinestone brooch, c. 1930s, **$165**.*

*Trifari brooches, 1930s-1940s, from left: sterling and rhinestones, **$185**; enameling, rhinestones and blue glass, **$195**; rhinestones, **$135**; rhinestones, **$130**.*

*Marcel Boucher bird brooch with enameling, opaque glass, clear and pink rhinestones, c.1930s, **$795**.*

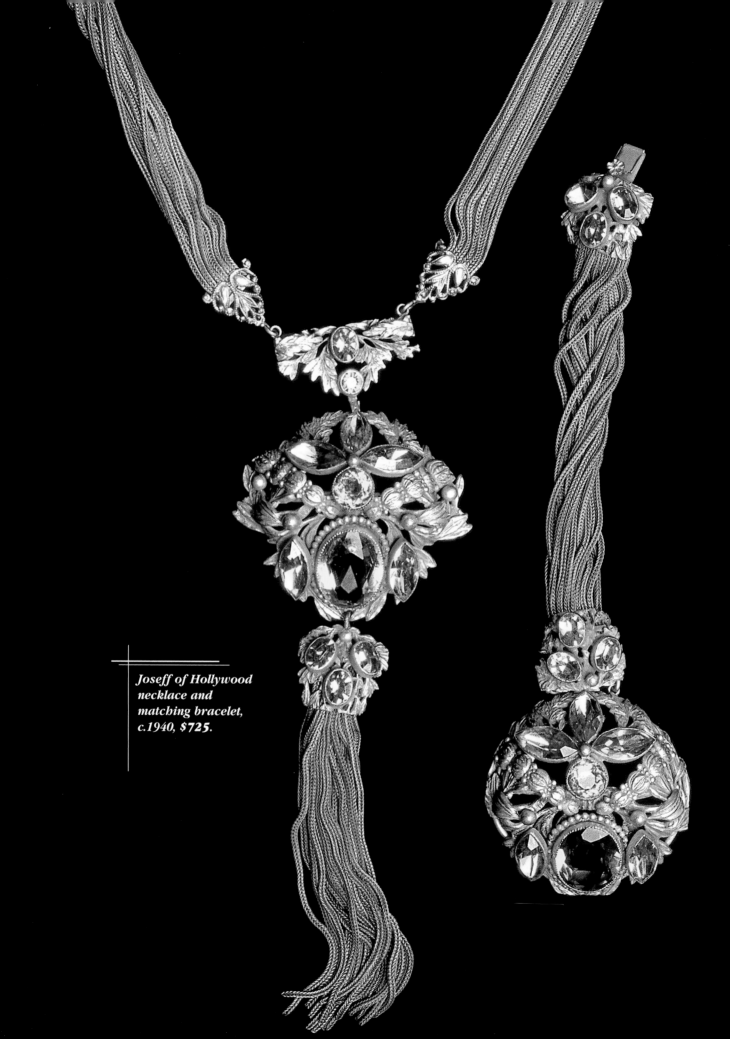

*Joseff of Hollywood
necklace and
matching bracelet,
c.1940, $725.*

*Left: Trifari fur clip with enameling and clear rhinestones, c. 1930s, **$195**; middle: Pennino floral brooch with amethyst glass, clear rhinestones and enameling, c. 1930s, **$345**; right: Mazer flower brooch with enameling and clear rhinestones, c. 1930s, **$245**.*

*Reja necklace, earring and bracelet set with rhinestones and open back rhinestones, c. 1950s, **$265**.*

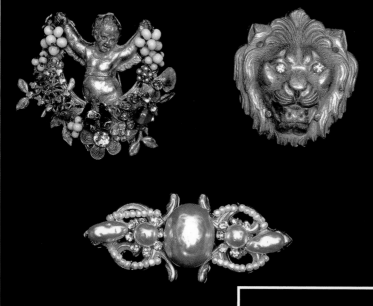

Miriam Haskell brooches, c. 1950s, clockwise from top left: cherub with blue, green and pink glass and rhinestones, $295; lion's head with rhinestones, $165; faux pearls and rhinestones, $185.

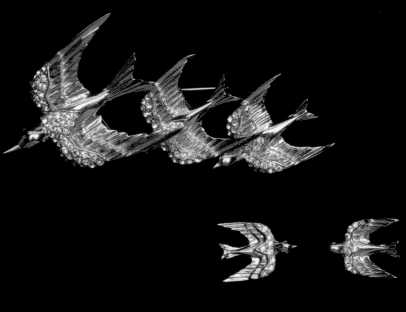

Coro sterling triplet with matching earrings, rhinestones, c. 1940s, $625.

Trifari brooch and earring set, rhinestones, c. 1965, $95.

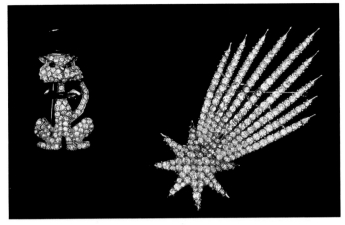

Left: Kramer of New York cat in a top hat brooch, rhinestones and enameling, c. 1950s, $95; right: Trifari starburst brooch, rhinestones, c. 1966, $150.

Eisenberg rhinestone brooch and earring set, c. 1940s, $325.

Warner rhinestone brooch and earring set, c. 1950s, $95.

Weiss brooch and earring set, rhinestones, c. 1950s, $165.

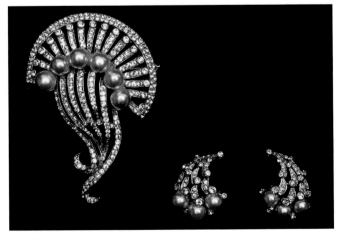

Left: Reja sterling brooch and earring set with rhinestones and faux pearls, c. 1940s, $395.

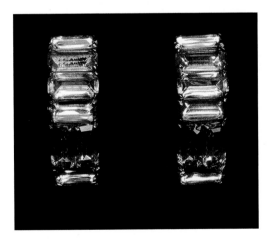

Eisenberg Original rhinestone dress clips, c. 1930s, $145.

Pennino sterling vermeil brooch with red and clear rhinestones, c. 1940s, $425.

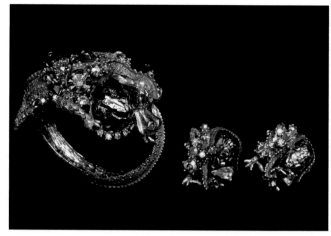

Har dragon cuff and earring set, blue aurora borealis and red aurora borealis rhinestones, c. 1950s, $695.

Left: Ciner brooch with pink glass, faux pearl, amethyst and light blue rhinestones, c. 1940, $345; right: De Rosa sterling vermeil fur clip with red glass and clear rhinestones, c. 1940s, $295.

Left: Chanel arrow brooch, pot metal and rhinestones, c.1930s, $825; right: Chanel flower brooch, pot metal with green glass and clear rhinestones, c.1930s, $700.

Trifari fur clips, c. 1930s, from left: enameling with green open back rhinestones and clear rhinestones, $425; clear rhinestones, $325.

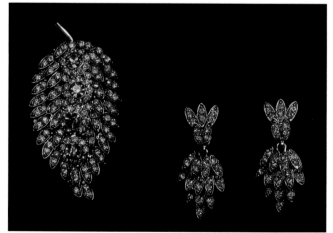

Hollycraft brooch and earring set, c. 1950s, $195.

NOVELTY JEWELRY

Celluloid pendant and chain with paint and blue and clear rhinestones, c. 1920, $325.

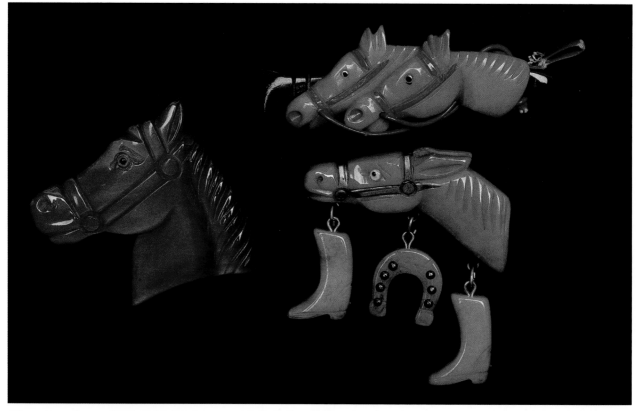

*Horse brooches, c. 1935-1945, left: butterscotch Bakelite, **$350**; top right: butterscotch and green Bakelite with red-leather accents, **$625**; bottom right: butterscotch Bakelite with metal accents, **$850**.*

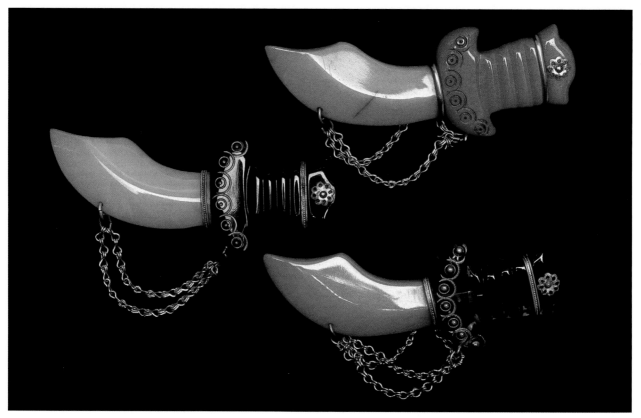

*Bakelite sword brooches, c. 1935-1945, **$525** each.*

*Left: Lucite and red Bakelite bird brooch, c. 1935-1945, **$185**; right: Lucite and green Bakelite horse brooch, c. 1935-1945, **$225**.*

*Left: red Bakelite anchor brooch with plastic charms, c. 1935-1940, **$495**; right: Bakelite military brooch with Bakelite drum charms, c. 1935-1940, **$650**.*

*Articulated butterfly brooch, green and marbled butterscotch Bakelite, c. 1940s, **$1200**.*

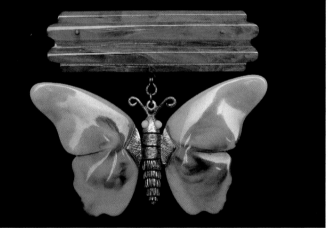

*Left: carved Bakelite rooster brooch, c. 1940, **$210**; right: Bakelite and wood nautical brooch, c. 1940s, **$350**.*

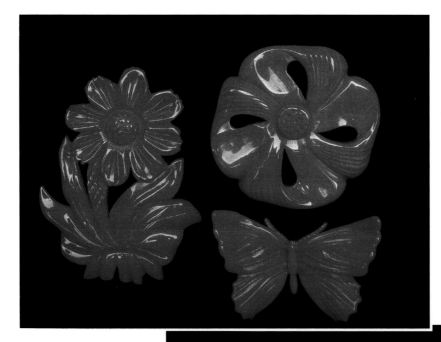

Left: carved red Bakelite flower brooch, c. 1940s, **$625**; top right: carved red Bakelite flower brooch, c. 1940s, **$325**; Bakelite butterfly buckle, c. 1935, **$85**.

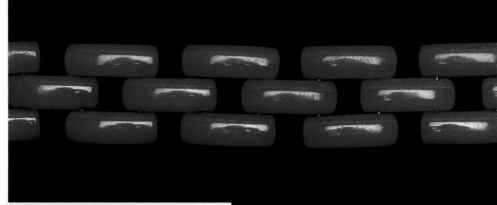

Red Bakelite link bracelet, c. 1940s, **$345**.

Applejuice and red Bakelite necklace, c. 1935, **$450**.

*Celluloid cameo
pendant and
chain, c. 1920-
1930, $195.*

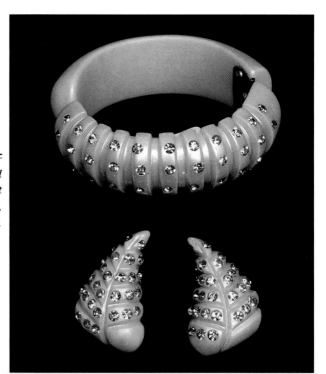

*Thermoplastic hinged bangle and earring set with blue rhinestones, c. 1950s, **$185**.*

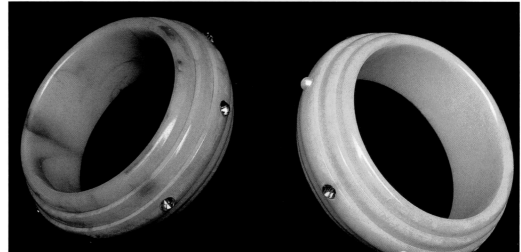

*Bakelite bangles with faux pearls, green, red, blue, topaz, and clear rhinestones, c. 1935-1945, **$575** each.*

*Celluloid and rhinestone bangles, c. 1925-1930, **$185-$225** each.*

*Bicycle brooch, leather and enameled metal, c. 1935, **$65**.*

*Leather figural brooch, c.1940-1945, **$85**.*

*Molded glass bead brooch, red, yellow, blue, and green glass beads, c. 1940s, **$95**.*

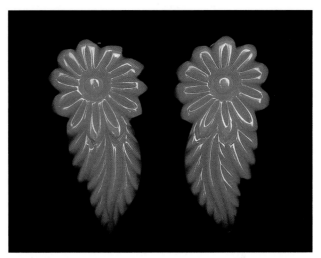

*Butterscotch Bakelite floral dress clips, c. 1940s, **$125**.*

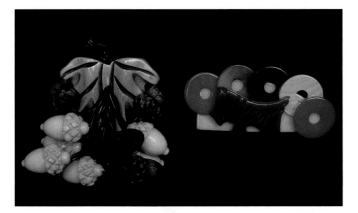

*Left: acorn brooch with Bakelite and wood, c. 1935-1945, **$425**; right: Bakelite Scottie dog brooch, c. 1935-1940, **$225**.*

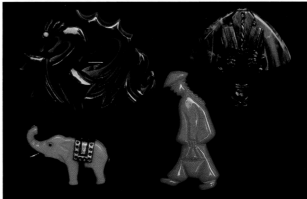

*Top left: green Bakelite dragon brooch, c. 1935-1945, **$950**; top right: green Bakelite and plastic figural brooch, c. 1940s, **$195**; bottom left: butterscotch Bakelite and silver elephant brooch, c. 1930s, **$195**; bottom right: orange Bakelite, Asian man figural brooch, c. 1935-1945, **$225**.*

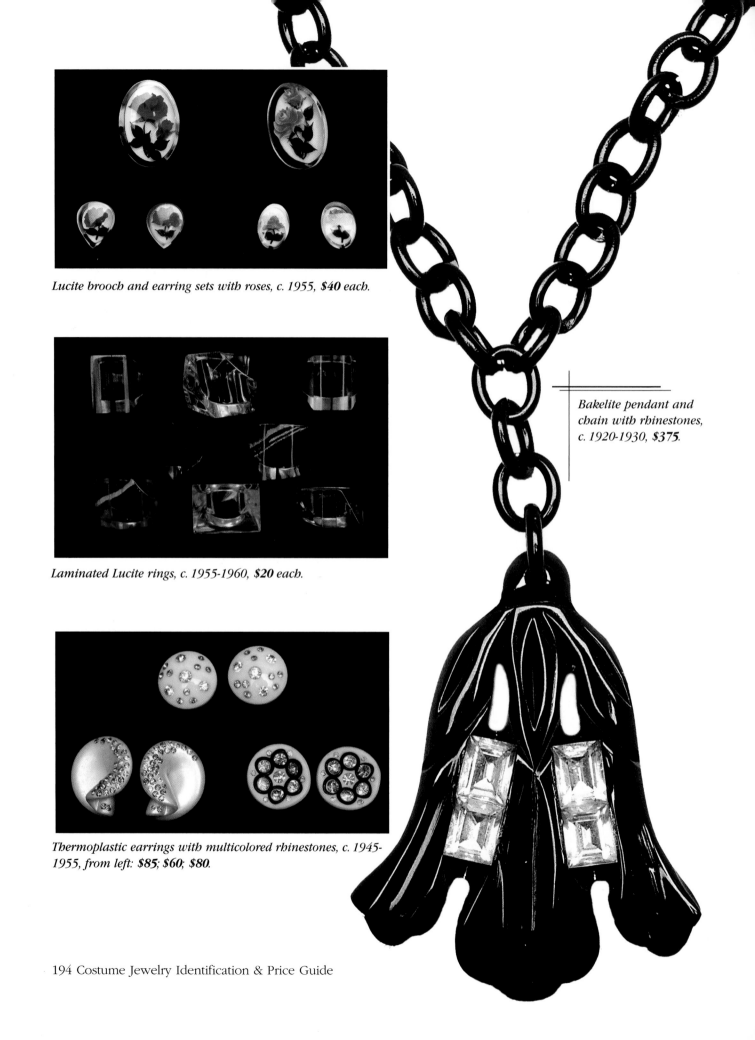

Lucite brooch and earring sets with roses, c. 1955, **$40** each.

Laminated Lucite rings, c. 1955-1960, **$20** each.

Thermoplastic earrings with multicolored rhinestones, c. 1945-1955, from left: **$85**; **$60**; **$80**.

Bakelite pendant and chain with rhinestones, c. 1920-1930, **$375**.

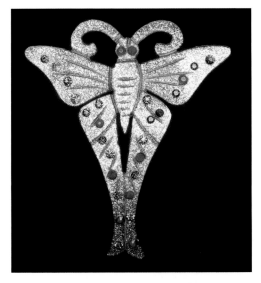

Celluloid butterfly brooch with red, green, blue, and topaz rhinestones, c. 1925, $165.

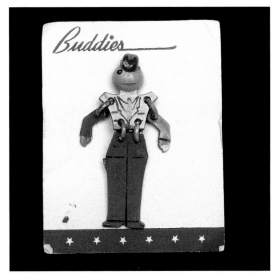

Military "Buddies" brooch on original card, plastic, c. 1940s, $245.

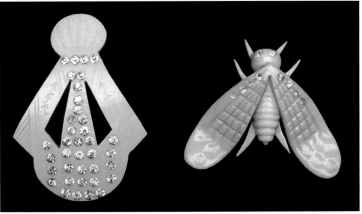

Celluloid brooches with rhinestones, c. 1920s, from left: art deco design, $85; bug, $165.

Applejuice Bakelite brooch with celluloid pharaoh cameo, c. 1930s, $195.

Patriotic wood brooch with Lucite blocks that spell out USA, c. 1940s, $265.

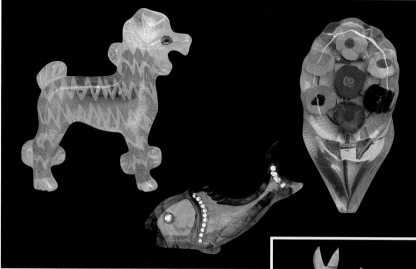

Left: reverse-carved Lucite dog brooch, c. 1935-1945, **$225**; middle: Lucite fish brooch with rhinestones, c. 1940s, **$65**; right: reverse-carved applejuice Bakelite dress clip, c. 1935-1945, **$195**.

Wooden dog brooches, c. 1940-1945, from left: **$45**; **$95**; **$85**.

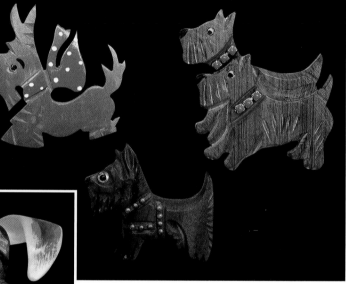

Left: wood and applejuice Bakelite turtle brooch, c. 1935-1945, **$225**; middle: wood Mountie brooch with google eyes, c. 1940, **$45**; right: hand-painted wood and Lucite dog brooch, c. 1935-1945, **$165**.

Wood dog brooches, c. 1940-1945, from left: **$95**; **$65**; **$75**.

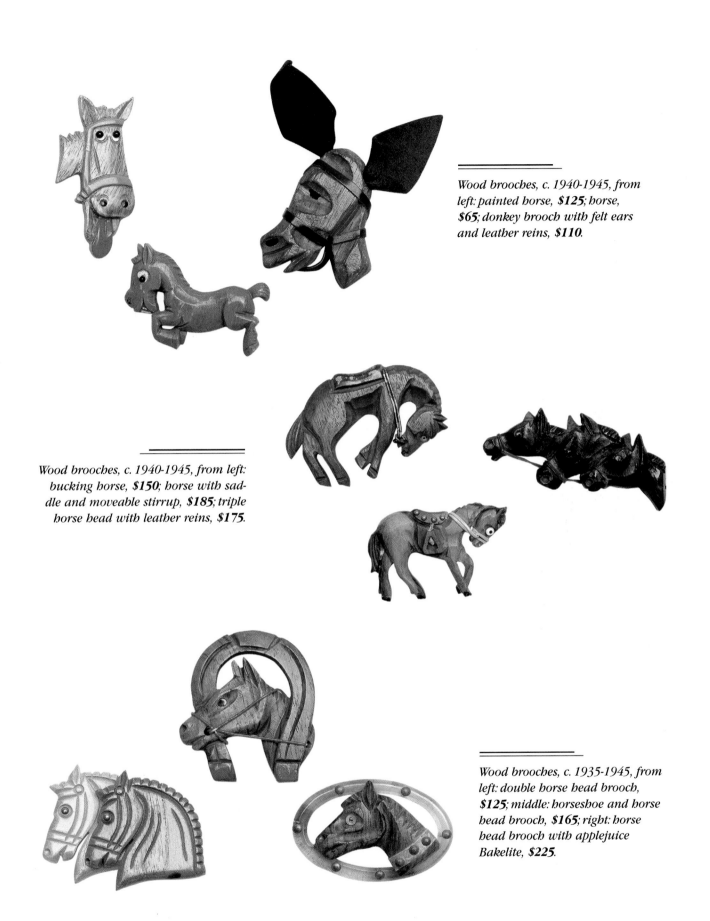

Wood brooches, c. 1940-1945, from left: painted horse, **$125**; horse, **$65**; donkey brooch with felt ears and leather reins, **$110**.

Wood brooches, c. 1940-1945, from left: bucking horse, **$150**; horse with saddle and moveable stirrup, **$185**; triple horse head with leather reins, **$175**.

Wood brooches, c. 1935-1945, from left: double horse head brooch, **$125**; middle: horseshoe and horse head brooch, **$165**; right: horse head brooch with applejuice Bakelite, **$225**.

Left: carved butterscotch Bakelite stretch bracelet, c. 1935-1945, **$295**; middle: carved red Bakelite bangle, c. 1935-1945, **$225**; right: carved butterscotch Bakelite bangle, c. 1935-1945, **$195**.

Left: black Bakelite bangle, c. 1935-1945, **$375**; middle: blue marbled Bakelite polka dot bangle, c. 1935-1945, **$850**; right: green Bakelite stretch bracelet, c. 1935-1945, **$150**.

Celluloid and rhinestone bangles, c. 1925-1930; **$100-$375** each.

*Left: Lucite and wood crab brooch, c. 1935-1945, **$145**; middle: Lucite and wood windmill brooch, c. 1935-1945, **$110**; right: wood and Lucite flower basket brooch, c. 1935-1945, **$145**.*

*Left: wood western boot brooch, c. 1940-1945, **$30**; right: wood saddle brooch, c. 1940-1945, **$35**.*

*Hand-painted wood elephant brooch with brass and red glass, c. 1940, **$110**.*

*Left: wood and applejuice Bakelite banjo brooch, c. 1940-1945, **$145**; hand-painted wood donkey and cart brooch with applejuice Bakelite, c. 1940-1945, **$125**; wood carpenter brooch, c. 1940-1945, **$75**.*

*Western design wood brooches, c. 1940-1945, from left, **$225**; **$150**.*

*Bakelite cameo brooches, c. 1935-1945, from left: black and butterscotch Bakelite, **$550**; butterscotch and black Bakelite, **$225**; red Bakelite, **$275**; butterscotch and applejuice Bakelite and brass accents, **$450**.*

*Left: green carved Bakelite brooch, c. 1935-1945, **$425**; middle: Bakelite fruit basket brooch, c. 1935-1945, **$475**; right: red Bakelite heart with green Bakelite balls, c. 1935-1945, **$375**.*

Wood elephant brooch, c. 1940, **$125**.

Lucite and Bakelite cameo brooches, c. 1940s, from left: **$125**; **$145**.

Bakelite bracelet with plastic cameo, c. 1935-1945, **$350**.

Left: carved black Bakelite dress clip, c. 1930s, **$95**; *middle: carved black Bakelite eagle brooch with red and clear rhinestones, c. 1935-1945,* **$450**; *carved black Bakelite bow brooch, c. 1935-1945,* **$675**.

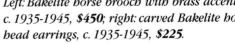
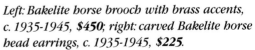

Left: Bakelite horse brooch with brass accents, c. 1935-1945, **$450**; *right: carved Bakelite horse head earrings, c. 1935-1945,* **$225**.

*Left: red and blue Bakelite earrings, c. 1935-1945, **$150**; right: green Bakelite earrings, c. 1935-1945, **$125**.*

*Brass necklace with carved green Bakelite leaf charms, c. 1935-1945, **$325**.*

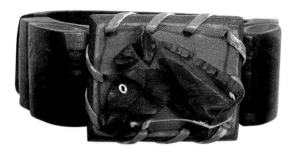

Clockwise from bottom left: green Bakelite ring, c. 1935-1945, **$145**; Bakelite prison ring, c. 1935-1945, **$225**; Bakelite prison ring with photo, c. 1935-1945, **$150**; Lucite ring with bug, c. 1955-1960, **$75**; Bakelite ring, c. 1935-1945, **$95**.

Hinged wood bangle with leather, c. 1940–1945, **$295**.

Left: chrome and end-of-day Bakelite brooch, c. 1935-1945, **$165**; right: chrome and green Bakelite, c. 1935-1945, **$295**.

Celluloid bracelet with Bakelite charms, c. 1940, **$225**.

Wood link necklace with horse pendant, c. 1940, **$295**.

Occupied Japan brooches, c. 1940s, from left: Snow White, **$95**; Scottie dog, **$65**; flower basket, **$45**.

MEXICAN

Sterling pendant with carved obsidian, Los Ballesteros, c. 1950s, $375.

*Sterling and stone flower basket brooch, William Spratling, c. 1940s, **$1200**.*

*Sterling brooch with aventurine quartz, Maricela, c. 1950s, **$225**.*

*Sterling pre-Hispanic design hinged cuff, c. 1950s, **$495**.*

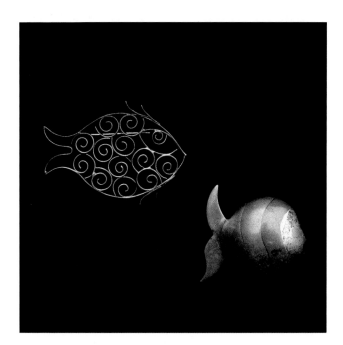

*Left: sterling fish brooch, c. 1955-1965, **$85**; right: metales casado fish brooch, c. 1950s, $115.*

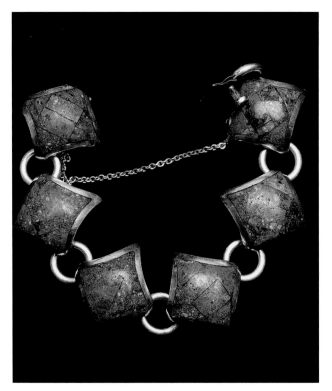

*Sterling bracelet with turquoise, c. 1960s, **$195**.*

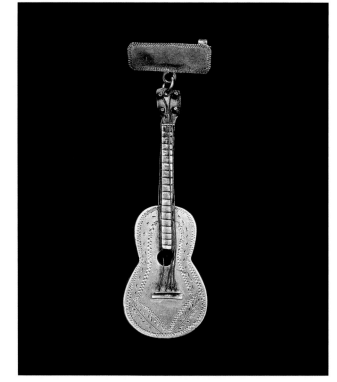

*Sterling guitar brooch, c. 1940s, **$150**.*

*Bernice Goodspeed sterling hinged bangle, c. 1950s, **$1000**.*

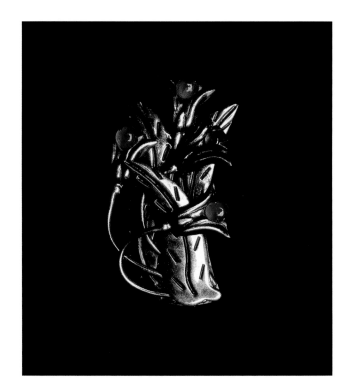

*Sterling brooch with amethysts, c. 1950s, **$185**.*

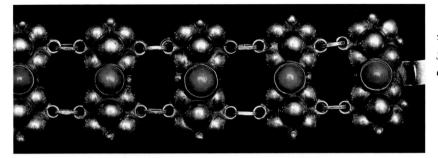

Sterling and turquoise bracelet, c. 1950, $195.

Top: sterling bracelet with obsidian, c. 1950s, $225; bottom: sterling and obsidian earrings, c. 1950s, $45.

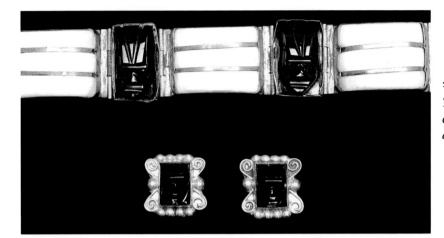

Top: Sterling bracelet, c. 1950s, $300; bottom: sterling bracelet, c. 1950s, $300.

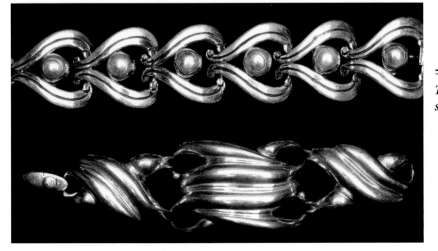

Top: sterling bracelet, c. 1955-1965, $185; sterling bracelet, c. 1980s, $145.

*Sterling bracelet, Maricela, 1955, **$325**.*

*Enameled bracelet, Margot de Taxco, c.1960s, **$425**.*

*Top: sterling pre-Hispanic design bracelet, c.1950s, **$195**; bottom: sterling bracelet, c. 1950s, **$165**.*

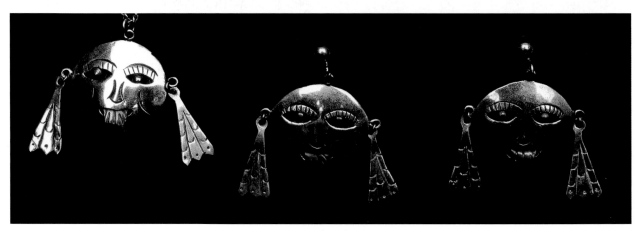

*Metales casado face design necklace and earring set, c. 1960s, **$295**.*

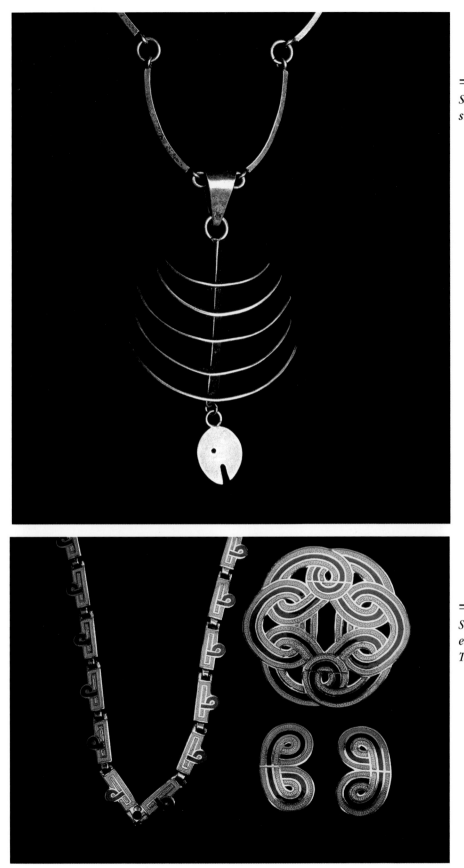

*Sterling necklace with fish pendant, signed EMV, c. 1960s, **$185**.*

*Sterling and enamel necklace, earrings, and brooch set, Margot de Taxco, c. 1950s, **$1500**.*

SCANDINAVIAN JEWELRY

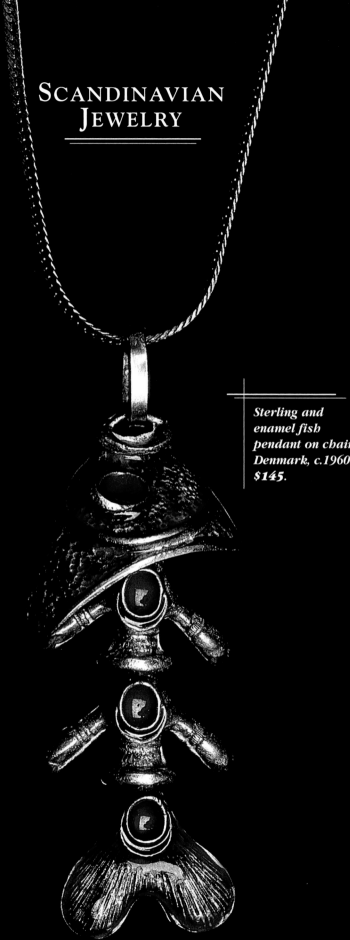

Sterling and enamel fish pendant on chain, Denmark, c.1960s, $145.

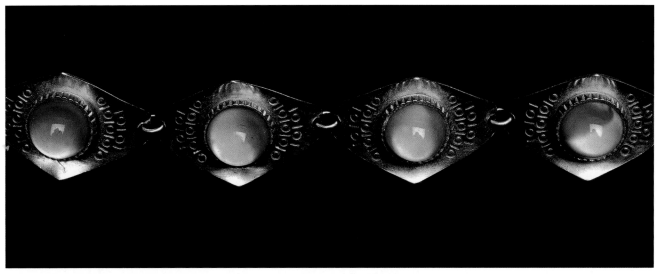

Scandinavian pewter bracelet with glass cabochons, c.1950s/1960s, $185.

Sterling and enamel butterfly necklace, designed by Volmar Bahner, c.1950s, $85.

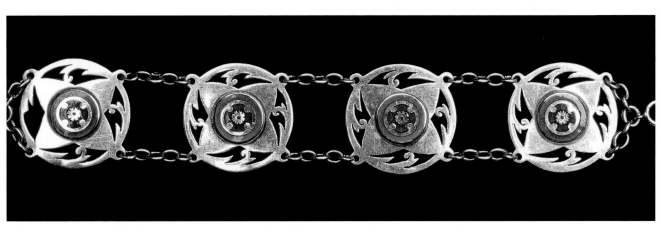

Sterling bracelet with enameling, Norway, c. 1940s, $425.

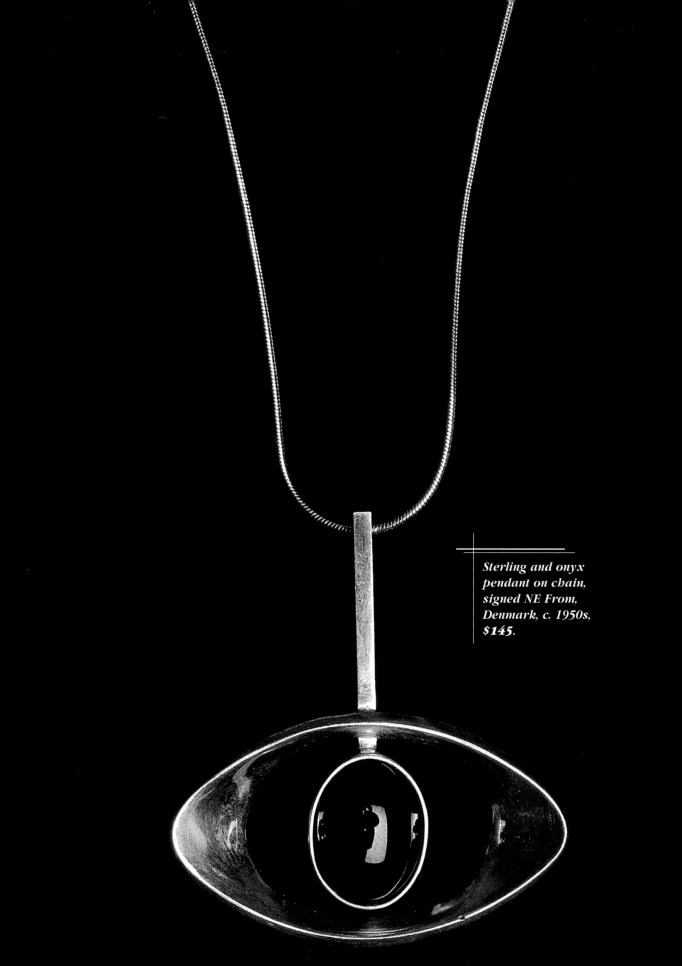

Sterling and onyx pendant on chain, signed NE From, Denmark, c. 1950s, $145.

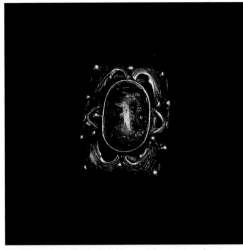

*Sterling handmade ring with green glass and fish design, Denmark, c.1970, **$300**.*

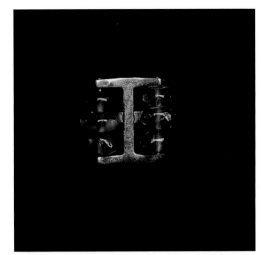

*Sterling ring with orange beads, c.1960s, **$185**.*

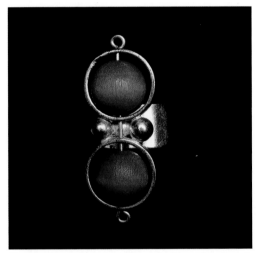

*Modern-design ring with wood beads, signed Aarikka, Finland, c. 1960s, **$95**.*

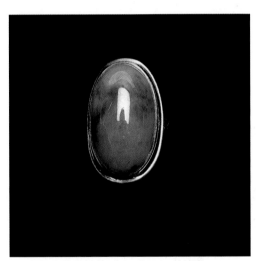

*Sterling ring, Sweden, c. 1950s, **$350**.*

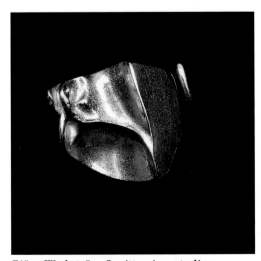

*Björn Weckström Sagitta ring, sterling, c.1970s, Finland, **$550**.*

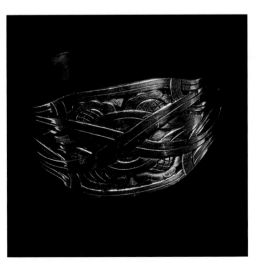

*Georg Jensen sterling cuff, Denmark, c. 1980s, **$750**.*

*Pewter pendant
with glass, signed
JØrgen Jensen,
Denmark, 1960s,
$125.*

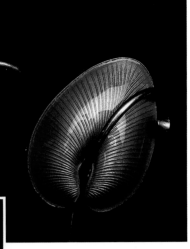

Sterling and enamel brooches, designed by Volmar Bahner, signed "VB," Denmark, c. 1950s, from left: $70; $110.

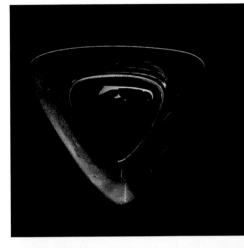

Left: sterling brooch with green glass, signed NE From, Denmark, c. 1950s, $95; right: sterling brooch, Denmark, c. 1940s, $85.

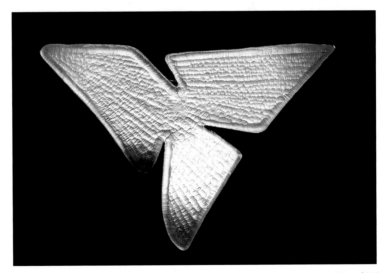

Sterling and enamel brooch, signed "J. Tostrup," Norway, c. 1950s, $95.

Brass and enamel brooch, Norway, c. 1950s, $195.

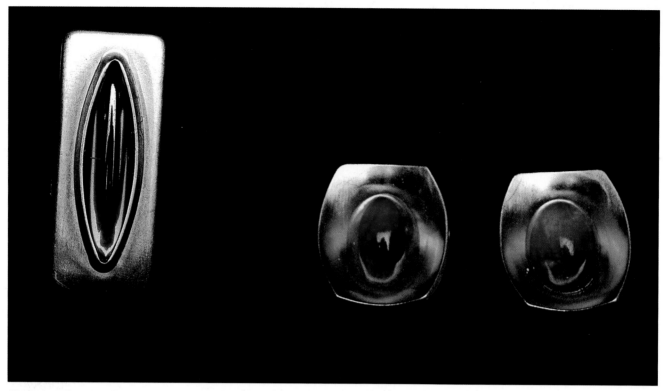

*Pewter and topaz glass ring and earring set, signed Jørgen Jensen, Denmark, c. 1950s, **$145**.*

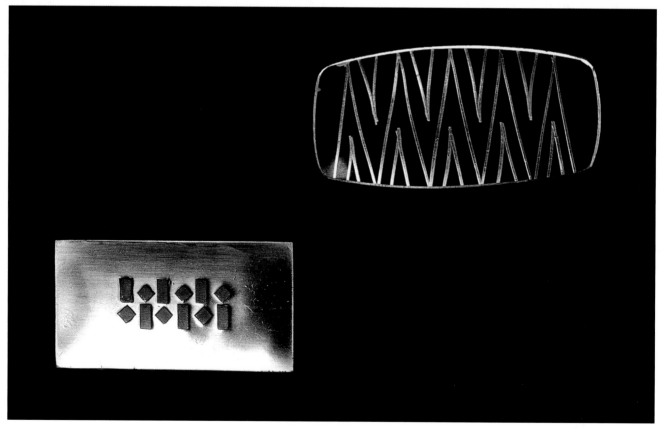

*Left: tin modern-design brooch, Denmark, c.1960s, **$85**; right: pewter and enamel brooch, signed "Jørgen Jensen, Denmark," c. 1960s, **$95**.*

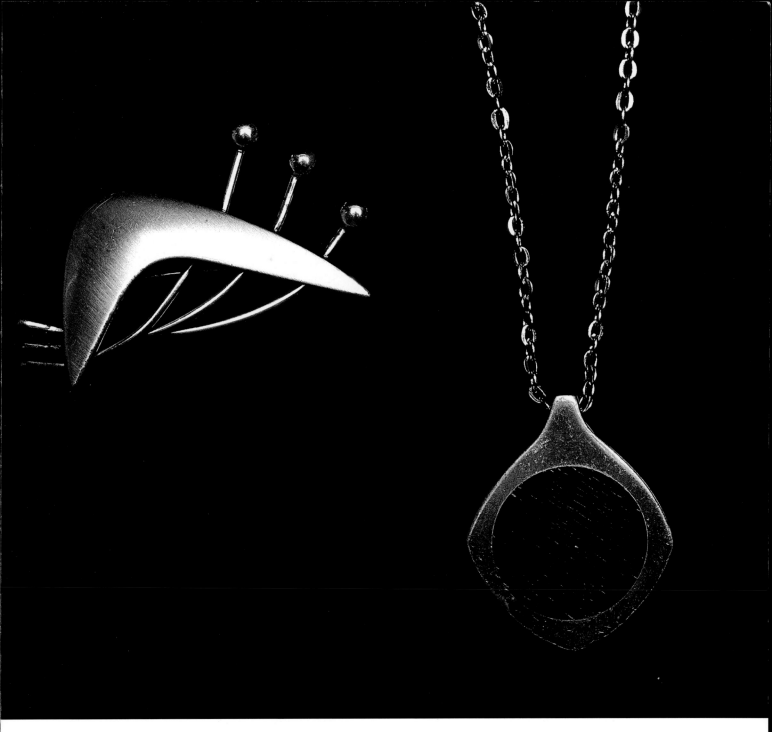

Sterling modern design brooch, Finland, c.1950s, $85; right: Scandinavian pewter and rosewood pendant on chain, c.1960s, $60.

Care of Costume Jewelry

Do not spray perfumes, deodorants, or hairsprays around rhinestone jewelry. The products will adhere to the stones, and will cause damage to them.

Do not store rhinestone jewelry for prolonged periods of time in plastic bags. Moisture will be trapped inside destroying the rhinestones.

Do not store rhinestone jewelry in hot areas or in direct sunlight. The heat will cause the glue to melt, and can also cause moisture to form that will destroy the rhinestones.

Do not store rhinestone jewelry on top of one another. The rhinestones are made from glass and can chip or crack.

Be careful when handling Bakelite and celluloid jewelry. While handling the jewelry does not cause a problem, when dropped onto a hard surface, the material can crack or break.

Pot metal is a soft material. Care must be taken not bend or crush it.

It is important to remember that a rhinestone has a foil back, which will become damaged when it is exposed to moisture. Never dip rhinestone jewelry in any kind of liquid. This will damage the piece. If you need to clean rhinestone jewelry, spread out a towel and lay the piece on the towel. Then using a clean, dry cosmetic brush, dust the piece off. If the stones seem cloudy, you can clean them with a household cleaner. To do this, dip a toothbrush into the cleaner and then tap off the excess liquid. Then brush the stones gently taking care not to get the liquid into the setting as it will destroy the foil backing and the rhinestone will lose its brilliance. After you have finished brushing the piece, turn it upside down onto the towel and let it dry for three to four hours before putting it away.

Do not put disintegrating pieces of celluloid jewelry near other pieces of celluloid. It will cause the other pieces to catch the "disease" and damage the pieces.

When handling the hand-woven hair jewelry, try to handle it by the findings, rather than the hair itself. The oil from your skin can cause damage to the hair.

Celluloid should be stored in a dry place.

Hallmarks

Hallmarks are a way of identifying a piece of jewelry's age and material. The hallmark can indicate the country of origin, the date of manufacture, and the metal content. Each country has a different system that it uses. There are books available that illustrate the different hallmarks.

British Hallmarks
Gold

Gold is hallmarked with a crown plus the carat.

In Scotland, from 1798 to 1975, gold was marked with a thistle.

In 1854, 9k, 12k and 15k gold were legalized.

In 1975, all gold hallmarks were made uniform with the crown hallmark and designation of fineness in the thousandths, the place of assay, and the date letter.

Silver

Silver was hallmarked with a lion passant, which designates sterling silver that is .925 fine.

In 1335, English law required silversmith's to imprint their hallmarks onto the silver.

In 1479, a letter signifying the year of manufacture was begun.

In Scotland, before 1975, the silver hallmark was a thistle.

Assay Hallmarks

Originally, the five assay offices were located in London, Birmingham, Sheffield, Edinburgh, and Chester (closed in 1962).

The London assay hallmark is a leopard's head.

The Birmingham assay hallmark is an anchor.

The Chester assay hallmark is a shield with a sword and sheaves of wheat.

Date Letter Hallmarks

A date letter hallmark is designated by a letter of the alphabet. Each letter is representative of a year. The years are differentiated by the font/style of the letter and the background upon which the letter rests.

A full cycle is A-Z.

To determine the year, you need to look up the letter and the shape of the background in a hallmark book.

Finland
Silver

The hallmark of a crown inside of a heart indicates that the piece was locally manufactured.

The hallmark of a crown inside an oval background indicates that the item was made for import.

French Hallmarks
Gold

Gold is hallmarked with an Eagle's head indicating 18k gold.

In 1912, platinum was stamped with a dog's head.

Silver

The Paris Assay office used the boar's head hallmark to indicate a fineness of 800 or more.

Outside of Paris, the crab hallmark was used.

Gold and Silver

After 1829, jewelry made of a combination of gold and silver were embossed with a connected boar's and eagle's head.

Maker's Hallmarks

After 1838, a maker's hallmark was required on gold and silver jewelry. This hallmark can be found inside a diamond-shaped background.

Mexican
Silver

The spread eagle hallmark was introduced after World War II.

Sweden
Silver

The hallmark of three crowns in a trefoil indicates that the piece was locally manufactured.

The hallmark of three crowns in an oval background indicates that the piece was manufactured for import.

The hallmark of an "S" in a hexagon indicates a fineness of 830 or more.

Bibliography

Bell, Jeanine. Answers to Questions About Old Jewelry, 6th Edition. Iola, WI: Krause Publications, 2003.

Brown, Marcia. Unsigned Beauties of Costume Jewelry. Paducah, KY: Collector Books, 2000.

Brown, Marcia. Signed Beauties of Costume Jewelry. Paducah, KY: Collector Books, 2000.

Brown, Marcia and Leigh Leshner. Hidden Treasures: Rhinestone Jewelry. Los Angeles, CA: Venture Entertainment Group, Inc., 1998.

Brown, Marcia and Leigh Leshner. Hidden Treasures: Signed Costume Jewelry Volumes 1-5. Los Angeles, CA: Venture Entertainment Group, Inc., 1998.

Dolan, Maryanne. Collecting Rhinestone & Colored Jewelry, 4th Edition. Iola, WI: Krause Publications, 1993.

Harranfor, Susan and Jim. 'Remembering A Loved One With Mourning Jewelry.' Antiqueweek. December 1997.

Keintz, Rene. "Bohemian Garnets: Seduce With Light Catching Color." Houston Chronicle. June 22, 2001.

Keintz, Rene. Ageless Look of Scottish Agate. Houston Chronicle. January 3, 2003.

Leshner, Leigh and Christie Romero. Hidden Treasures: A Collector's Guide to Antique and Vintage Jewelry of the 19th and 20th Centuries. Los Angeles, CA: Venture Entertainment Group, Inc., 1992.

Matlins, Antoinette. Jewelry & Gems: The Buying Guide. Woodstock, VT: Gemstone Press, 1997.

Miller, Anna. The Buyer's Guide To Affordable Antique Jewelry. New York, NY: Citadel Press, 1993.

Rezazadeh, Fred. Collectible Silver Jewelry. Paducah, KY: Collector Books, 2001.

Romero, Christie. Warman's Jewelry. Iola, WI: Krause Publications, 2002.

Tucker, Andrew and Tamsin Kingswell. Fashion: A Crash Course. New York, NY: Watson-Guptill Publications, 2000.

About the Author

A vintage jewelry collector since her preteens, Leigh Leshner shares her interest by co-writing and producing the award-winning Hidden Treasures video series through her own film/television/video production company, Venture Entertainment Group, Inc. She participates in antiques shows and provides appraisal services. Leigh has also been a dealer for more than 12 years and sells jewelry through her website, Thanks for the Memories (www.tias.com/stores/memories/). She is the author of Vintage Jewelry: A Price and Identification Guide, 1920-1940s, and Rhinestone Jewelry: A Price and Identification Guide, published by Krause Publications.

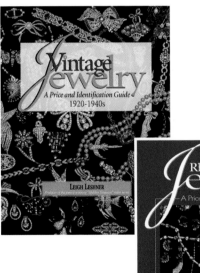

Index